Nailing Jelly to a Tree

Nailing Jelly to a Tree

Jerry Willis and
William Danley, Jr.

dilithium Press
Beaverton, Oregon

ISBN: 0-918398-42-8
Library of Congress catalog card number: 80-68566

Printed in the United States of America.

dilithium Press
P. O. Box 606
Beaverton, Oregon 97075

Preface

By the time most books are written and edited the authors are so sick of working with the manuscript they never want to see it again. As this preface is written, that's exactly how we feel. Humans, though, have remarkable recuperative powers. Once the memories of late-nite writing sessions, working Saturdays stolen from homecoming parties and football games, and Sunday afternoons without Hollywood Henderson and the cheery face of Bum Phillips dim a little, we hope our attitude will gradually change. Perhaps we will even begin to feel a warm glow about the book. At least there will be stories to tell the grandchildren.

We called this book *Nailing Jelly to a Tree* because learning about software is a lot like nailing jelly to a tree. Software is nebulous, and difficult to get a firm grasp on. Taking those first steps toward becoming the master of your computer's software is like trying to nail jelly to a tree. It can be done, but it isn't easy. We would like to thank Bill Blake for suggesting the title.

Appreciation is also expressed to Bill Ferreira, Lu Isett, Karl Kluthe, Martin Kennedy, Virgie Nolte, Marci Steen, Don Tanner, and Reggie Ukwuije who read and offered suggestions on some of the chapters. Two students at Texas Tech University, Cleora Boyd and Debra Arminderiz, worked diligently on several sections of the book and made many useful contributions. A special thanks is expressed to Debbie who critically read all the chapters. Her efforts and suggestions made it a better book. This book is dedicated to her and to all those like Debbie who, while not fanatics on the topic, allow computers a place in their life and in their work.

Contents

Chapter 1

Introduction to the Care and Feeding of Small Computers

It is beginning to look like everyone and their hound dog is writing at least one book on small computers. A typical catalog from one of the mail order suppliers will list between 100 and 200 books that are relevant to microprocessors, and such a list won't include the 900 or more books on related topics and those written specifically for university courses on microcomputers.

The abundance of books today is a far cry form the sparce selection available a few years ago. In the early seventies enthusiasts could afford to buy every personal computing book that was printed and still not have to brown bag lunch. In those days we were willing to buy anything because even a poorly written book, or one written for the professional engineer, would have some useful information. And information on small computers was in short supply back then.

Today, however, in this time of plenty, it behooves all readers to carefully select the books they buy. And it becomes much more important for the writer of a book about small computers to help the reader make an intelligent selection. One "everything you ever wanted to know" book may be written for the professional engineer, for example, and may assume the reader has a great deal of basic electronics knowledge. Another book that covers the same topics may be written on the premise that the reader has no background in electronics or computer science. Both books may be good for a particular group of readers and terrible for others. In the following sections of this chapter I'll try to give you a feel for this book — who it was written for, and what it attempts to teach.

WHO IS THIS BOOK FOR?

Nailing Jelly to a Tree was written for the person who has a personal computer and is generally familiar with how it works (e.g. how to turn it on, load in a program, and make it go). The book's focus is on the various types of software in common use. It is assumed that the reader has at least a passing knowledge of computer hardware. Words that describe the different types of memory, for example, are used in this text without completely explaining them first. If ROM, RAM, and EPROM mean nothing to you it might be best to read a book like *Peanut Butter and Jelly Guide to Computers,* available from dilithium Press. Another alternative would be to buy a glossary of computer terms such as *Home Computers: A Beginner's Glossary and Guide,* also from dilithium. The glossary and guide begins with a brief introduction, but most of the book is in glossary form — you can look up terms that are unfamiliar to you. Unfamiliar terms are most likely to crop up while you're reading the chapters on machine and assembly language programming. The chapters on BASIC can be read with understanding even if you are totally unfamiliar with computer hardware.

As "appliance computers" such as the PET, Radio Shack's TRS-80, Apple, and Texas Instrument's small system become more and more popular there will be an increasing number of users who treat the computer just as they would a sophisticated TV game or kitchen appliance. That is, they will want to do no more than buy the cartridge or the cassette tape of a program they like, take it home, and put it in their computer. This book is not for that group since it requires very little skill or technical expertise to use a computer at the appliance level. At the other end of the continuum there are many computer freaks who want to spend most of their time writing programs and building equipment. The book was not written for that group either, although it might be useful as a beginning point if the erstwhile programmer has little or no experience.

Just who, then, is this book written for? It is for the person who is interested in using and adapting the thousands of computer programs that are available today in books, magazines, and from the mushrooming number of software houses that sell their wares to individuals and small businesses. In most instances a program in a magazine, or anywhere else for that matter, will be written for a particular computer, often not yours. That means it will require some modification before it works at your house. Being able to modify, enhance, change, and experiment with all the free and inexpensive programs that are now available requires a significant amount of software expertise, but not nearly the amount needed to take an idea and create a completely new program. Using someone else's program, lets you have the enjoyment of working with the computer without all the brain warping drudgery that is involved in writing a lengthy program. And, in fact, by carefully studying good programs and understanding how they operate you lay an excellent foundation for future programming work of your own.

WHAT YOU WILL READ ABOUT

To become a flexible and inventive program user it is necessary to master a number of areas of basic computer knowledge. Chapter 2, for example, covers the ins and outs of computer math and logic. The number systems used in programming are not difficult to learn; some say learning them is more tedious than difficult. They are essential building blocks, however, and Chapter 2 covers the most important number systems (decimal, binary, hexadecimal, and octal) as well as computer logic and common codes.

Chapter 3 introduces the reader to the various types of software in common use and to the software jargon that seems to flow so freely in our field. The jargon, like number systems, is not that complicated. Many words do, however, take on a specialized meaning when used in discussing software. Chapter 3 will help you follow the patter of that fast talking computer salesperson. Magazine articles, advertisements, and software instruction manuals all become a little less foreign when the jargon isn't a barrier to understanding.

The remaining chapters in the book are all concerned with one of the three major types of computer languages. Chapter 4 is devoted to the use of machine language while Chapter 5 deals with assembly language. These two chapters are not intended to make you a skilled programmer in two easy lessons. The purpose, instead, is to provide the beginner with information needed to understand and use programs written in machine or assembly language. A secondary goal, however, is to enable the reader to write short programs or to create subroutines that do a particular job. Such tasks are often needed and frequently avoided by beginning programmers because they view machine and assembly language programming as difficult tasks fraught with potential hazards and problems.

The final four chapters of the book deal with BASIC, the most popular higher level language for small computers. Chapters 6 and 7 cover the essentials of BASIC. Any person who wants to begin working immediately in that language should read these chapters first. Chapters 8 and 9 deal with converting and adapting existing BASIC programs so that they will run on your computer.

For readers who plan to use only one level of language (e.g., only higher level languages) it may be sufficient to read Chapters 1, 2, and 3 and then concentrate on the other chapter or chapters that are concerned with the type of programming that is the primary interest.

As you read this book keep in mind that understanding the principles involved is more important than memorizing the details. If you understand how something is done, it is always possible to look up the detailed information you need. This book has been purposely written at a moderate pace to encourage understanding. Important concepts are repeated and reviewed in different contexts throughout the book. In addition, wherever possible we have tried to teach concepts through examples and applications rather than as abstract principles. Many of the details have been organized and placed in convenient tables, charts, and appendices. There is no need, for example, to try and memorize the ASCII codes for letters and numbers. In the beginning you will find yourself looking up ASCII codes, machine language instruction codes, or BASIC commands frequently. These details are best learned, however, by use.

LEVELS OF COMPUTER LANGUAGE

It has already been mentioned that there are three levels of computer languages. Each has its major advantages and disadvantages; each has a pot full of terms and buzz words that are sprinkled through a programmer's conversation regardless of the level used. In the final section of this chapter the three levels will be introduced and discussed briefly.

Machine Language

In actual fact, computers speak only one language—machine language. Machine language is not, however, a single language. Each computer has its own set of instructions that are built into it by the designers. Instructions written in any other machine language must be translated into the machine language used by your computer before it can understand and process the instructions.

Just what is an instruction set? And how do computers use it? Inside the tiny microprocessor chip that is the heart of most small computers there is a maze of electronic connections that were formed when the chip was made. The pins on the outside of the package that houses the computer chip are simply the links between the chip and the rest of the computer. When the power is turned on, the chip will accept instructions on the *input pins*. Each instruction a chip understands has a number. If, for example, the number 3A is sent to a computer with an 8080 chip it would interpret it as an instruction to load the accumulator with the contents of a memory location that follows the instruction. Yes, 3A is a number; it will be discussed in Chapter 2. The *accumulator* is just a special storage location inside the computer chip.

Machine language programs take the relatively simple-minded instructions like 3A that are understood by the computer and make them do fancy things like payroll accounting or computer assisted instruction. Programming in machine language brings the user in direct contact with the computer, and the instructions used are understood and acted upon without any translation. Few people, however, choose machine language for major software development. Program development at this level is very long and involved from the programmer's point of view. Even something simple like adding two numbers takes several instructions. Machine language programs are also hard to correct, and generally can only be used in computers with CPU's that are very similar to the one for which they were developed.

Assembly Language

One of the most trying things about machine language programming is the fact that the symbols used for the instructions are numbers which give the programmer no indications of their meaning. Unless you memorize the numbers and their meanings, programming can be a slow process that is frequently punctuated by searches through the table of instruction codes. Programming in assembly language is one way of avoiding the problem of instruction labels that are not self-explanatory. Assembly language uses essentially the same grammar and syntax rules as a machine language, and the vocabulary is equivalent. Instead of a number, however, each instruction has a short mnemonic that provides a clue as to its function. As mentioned earlier, the machine code for the instruction to load data into the 8080 accumulator is 3A in machine language. In 8080 assembly language 3A becomes LDA (for Load A). That is much easier to remember.

Some programmers code their programs in assembly language and, once the program is written, they make the conversion to machine language by hand. Although it adds an extra step, many feel progress is faster when the initial work can be done with instruction labels that can be understood by the programmer. Again it should be pointed out, however, that the computer always works in the machine language no matter what language the programmers uses. There must always be some means of transforming the program into machine codes if it has not been written in machine language in the first place.

It is now possible to buy an *assembler* program for most of the small computers currently on the market. An assembler does the job of converting assembly language programs to machine code. Writing programs in assembly language has many advantages, especially when compared to working with machine language. It is easier to learn, easier to use, and quicker than machine language work for beginning programmers. A disadvantage is the fact that the assembler is itself a program which requires a system with enough memory to run it. That is probably a minor problem for most considering the delightful fall of memory prices lately. Once a program is assembled it will run in a computer just like any other machine language program, and it will take up far less memory space than the same program written in BASIC or any other high level language.

High Level Languages

Higher level languages will be discussed in Chapter 3, and the most popular of this group, BASIC, is the focus of the final four chapters of the book.

Simply put, a higher level language is a language whose instructions are easy for the programmer to understand. BASIC, for example, has the following instructions: PRINT, INPUT, and STOP. Using these instructions allows the programmer to tell the program what it is supposed to do. PRINT will cause whatever appears after it to be printed; INPUT X tells the computer to input a number and assign it to X. If the number 65 is entered, X will equal 65 after the INPUT X instruction. STOP tells the computer to stop executing when it reaches the end of the program.

The close correlation of the instruction labels and the action performed is a primary characteristic of higher level languages. Another characteristic is the power of each single instruction. If we want to add two numbers, divide the sum by a third number, and then print the quotient on the screen it requires only one line of instruction in BASIC:

$$PRINT\ A + B/C$$

To accomplish the same thing in a machine or assembly language would require many, many more instructions. The direct syntax and the power of the individual instructions are why languages like BASIC are used by well over 95% of the programmers who work with small computers.

Chapter 2

Two, Four, Six, Eight —
What You Gonna
Accumulate?

Math was never my strong point in high school, and as you might expect, it was not on my list of slick things to do on a Saturday afternoon either. Two more years of college math and another set of statistics courses in graduate school did absolutely nothing to enhance the subject's image in my eyes, and I will probably always prefer a well turned phrase to an elegant formula.

Like it or not, however, some knowledge of advanced math is necessary if you are to get the most from your computer. The silver lining in this otherwise dark cloud is the fact that the *advanced* math you will need is not really that complicated — different but not complicated.

In this chapter we'll begin with a discussion of binary numbers, the only type used inside the microcomputer. Next comes hexadecimal and octal, the number systems used by programmers. These number systems are easier for people to understand and use, but the computer must convert them to binary before they can be processed.

Once you have these basic number systems under your belt, the joys of Boolean algebra come next. This branch of algebra is used extensively in computer programming and in the design of computer logic circuits. The chapter ends with a discussion of the ASCII code. This chapter provides more detail than is necessary for the beginner. Much of it, in fact, will only be of use after some hands-on experience at the computer keyboard. I would suggest then, that the beginner read this chapter selectively. Read the material on binary math up to binary subtraction without borrowing. Then skip to the heading "Types of

Numbers" which deals with hexadecimal and octal numbers, among other things. Then read the material on Boolean algebra and the final few pages of Chapter 2 which discusses computer codes.

THE BINARY NUMBER SYSTEM

Most people go through their lives aware of only one number system, decimal. Decimal is a *base ten* system that used the *carry* or *place value* principle to represent quantities larger than 9. The decimal number 648, for example, is generally understood to mean:

$$6 \quad \text{hundreds}$$

$$4 \quad \text{tens}$$

$$8 \quad \text{ones}$$

Now consider the decimal number 222. The value of the right-most 2 is two times 1 or two. The adjacent 2 stands for two times ten or 20 while the third 2 stands for two times 100 or 200. There is a general principle in all this. Decimal numbers increase in value by a multiple of 10 each time they are shifted one position to the left. Thus the decimal system can represent extremely large values using only ten numerals (0, 1, 2, 3, 4, 5, 6, 7, 8, 9). Why are decimal or base 10 numbers so popular? It probably has a lot to do with the fact that humans have 10 fingers. Had the good Lord or evolution seen fit to give us six digits on each hand we probably would use a base 12 rather than base 10 system.

Because of our frequent contact with decimal numbers, they are easily understood and manipulated by most adults. Unfortunately, they give computers a bad case of indigestion. At its simplest level a computer can represent only two conditions. A memory chip, for example, is made up of many *cells,* each of which is capable of storing a small charge. Each cell is *on* or *off,* charged or uncharged, or whatever you want to label the two possible conditions. Generally the *on* condition is called a *1* or *true* while the *off* condition is designated a *0* or *false.*

Binary numbers are ideally suited to computers since they use only two numerals (1 and 0). Like decimal numbers, binary numbers make use of the place value concept in order to represent large numbers. The difference in binary, however, lies in the value given each position in a number. Figure 2-1 illustrates how place value is determined for a standard decimal number.

To determine the quantity represented, each digit in the number 100 is multiplied by a power of 10. The rightmost or least significant digit is multiplied by 10 to the 0 power or 1, while the 1 adjacent to it is multiplied by 10 to the first power or 10. The result of this process on the decimal number 1010 is illustrated below:

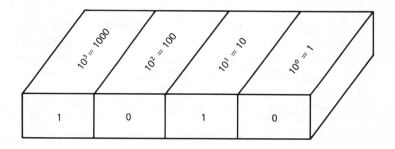

Figure 2-1   Place value for decimal numbers

$$
\begin{array}{rll}
1 \text{ times } 1000 = & 1000 \\
0 \text{ times } \ \ 100 = & \ \ \ \ 0 \\
1 \text{ times } \ \ \ 10 = & \ \ \ 10 \\
0 \text{ times } \ \ \ \ 1 = & \ \ \ \ 0 \\
\hline
\text{Total} = & 1010 \text{ decimal}
\end{array}
$$

It may seem silly to go through this process with a decimal number since you could just as easily have read the number correctly without all that razzle dazzle. The same process, however, applies to binary numbers, and you will find them much more difficult to read in the beginning. Figure 2-2 illustrates the process for the binary number 1010. Remember, 1010 binary (b) is not the same as 1010 decimal (d)!

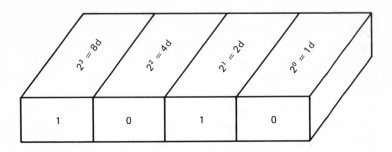

Figure 2-2   Place value for binary numbers

As the figure shows, each digit in a binary number is multiplied by a power of two rather than ten. A one in the rightmost or least significant position of a binary number is multiplied by 2 to the 0 power (2^0 equals 1 in decimal) while a one in the adjacent position is multiplied by 2 to the 1 power (2^1 equals 2 in the decimal). Here is how the binary number 1010 is broken down:

$$1 \text{ times } 8d = 8d$$
$$0 \text{ times } 4d = 0d$$
$$1 \text{ times } 2d = 2d$$
$$\underline{0 \text{ times } 1d = 0d}$$
$$\text{Total} = 10d$$

In the case of a binary number, however, the answers have been converted to decimal numbers since they are easier for most people to understand. Thus 1010b (the b stands for binary) is the same as 10d (d stands for decimal). It is important to note here that 1010b and 10d are both perfectly legitimate ways of expressing or signifying the same quantity, just as the French word pomme and the English word apple both describe the same thing.

This is a good point in the discussion to summarize the binary number system. It uses only two digits; it relies on the place value method so that the value of a digit increases by a power of two as it is moved from right to left. Binary numbers, like decimal numbers, can be of any length. When working with small computers, however, binary numbers with eight digits will generally be the standard. Most of the current crop of systems arrange their memory into *bytes*. Each byte can store one eight bit binary number. The binary number 00110101 can be placed in one byte of memory, and each of its eight *1's* and *0's* occupies one bit. The bits are often referred to by number. Bit 0 is the *least significant bit* or the one on the far right. Bit 7 is the *most significant bit* or the one on the far left.

Table 2-1 illustrates the relationship between binary and decimal numbers. In both decimal and binary *nothing* is a 0. The first numeral in both systems is 1, but the similarity stops there. Add 1 and 1 in decimal and you get 2. In binary the addition of 1 and 1 is 10. In binary, 10 means *1 two and 0 ones.* As Table 2-1 shows it takes a five digit binary number (10000) to represent the decimal number 16.

Table 2-1   Table of Binary and Decimal Values

binary	decimal	binary	decimal
1 =	1		
10 =	2	1000000000 =	512
100 =	4	10000000000 =	1024
1000 =	8	100000000000 =	2048
10000 =	16	1000000000000 =	4096
100000 =	32	10000000000000 =	8192
1000000 =	64	100000000000000 =	16384
10000000 =	128	1000000000000000 =	32768
100000000 =	256	10000000000000000 =	65536

Since we are dealing with 8 bit microprocessors it would be interesting to see how big a decimal number can be expressed by an eight bit binary number:

1	1	1	1	1	1	1	1	Binary Number
128	64	32	16	8	4	2	1	Decimal Value
255	127	63	31	15	7	3	1	Decimal Total

The table lists the decimal values of a binary 1 in each of eight positions, and the largest decimal value which could be expressed by a binary number with 1 to 8 bits. The five bit binary number 10000, for example, is equal to 16 decimal (d). The five bit binary number 11111 is equal to 31d and 31 is thus the largest value that can be expressed with a five bit binary number. With an eight bit binary number, a total of 256 different decimal values (0 to 255) can be expressed.

Since the computer uses binary numbers to perform house-keeping chores as well as actual work, the special characteristics of the binary number system determine, to some extent, the capacity and limitations of the computer. Most small computers, for example, set aside 16 pins on the computer chip to which 16 address lines are connected. These are used to indicate which memory *address* a piece of data is to be sent to or retrieved from. Thus any combination of 16 *ones and zeros* can be used to indicate a particular address in the computer. There are 65,536 possible patterns of zeros and ones on the 16 lines. The lowest memory location in a computer is assigned the address 0000 0000 0000 0000 while 1111 1111 1111 1111 is the address of the highest usable memory address (the spaces between the digits are for your ease in reading the number — they do not occur in actual numbers). In actual microcomputers the 16 bits of an address are generally broken into two 8 bit bytes to allow the computer to work with binary numbers with no more than 8 bits. The computer indicates a *one* is on a line by placing a high logic signal on an address pin, and the address line connected to it. A *zero* is indicated by placing a low signal on the line. In most microcomputers a logic high will be around 5V, and a logic low will be around 0V (ground). If the computer puts 0000 1000 0100 0000 on the address lines, and signals that it wants to read the information stored in that memory location, it would be reading from the location whose address is 2112. Here's how you can read the decimal equivalent of 0000 1000 0100 0000 to get 2,112:

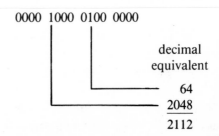

In addition to memory addresses, some small computers use 8

lines to select I/O ports through which data is sent or received. Suppose your keyboard has a binary address of 00000001 while a printer has address 00000010. The decimal address of the keyboard would be *1* while the printer address would be *2*. A total of 256 different devices could be given separate addresses using 8 lines.

BINARY MATH

Addition

Suppose there are two binary numbers which must be added. The rules for adding in binary are actually very simple:

Rule 1: zero + zero = zero

Rule 2: one + zero = one

Rule 3: zero + one = one

Rule 4: one + one = zero and carry one (usually to the next column)

Rule 5: one + one + one (e.g. a carry one) = one and carry one

Here are some examples of binary addition and their decimal equivalents:

	Binary	Decimal
	1	1
	+1	+1
	10	2
	10101101	173
	+01110110	+118
	100100011	291

Binary Subtraction and Negative Numbers

Most microprocessors today have the ability to subtract binary numbers through the use of one of the instructions built into the microprocessor chip. Computers that use the Z-80 microprocessor, for example, have an instruction (95 hex) that subtracts the value stored in register L from the value stored in

the accumulator. There are several other instructions that perform binary subtraction on numbers stored in various locations.

To subtract in binary requires some thought about how this
number system is actually set up. The rules for subtracting are
the same as for decimal subtracting as long as no borrowing is
involved:

Rule 1: zero − zero = zero

Rule 2: one − zero = one

Rule 3: one − one = zero

Let's try some examples which don't require borrowing:

$$\begin{array}{r} 11 \\ -\ 1 \\ \hline 10 \end{array} \qquad \begin{array}{r} 10 \\ -10 \\ \hline 0 \end{array} \qquad \begin{array}{r} 1101 \\ -\ 100 \\ \hline 101 \end{array}$$

Remember, all the examples above are binary, not decimal.

Now let's try a simple borrowing problem. Compare it to the
decimal equivalent next to it:

binary	decimal

$$\begin{array}{r} 10 \\ -1 \\ \hline 1 \end{array} \qquad\qquad \begin{array}{r} 2 \\ -1 \\ \hline 1 \end{array}$$

In the binary example, the zero in the right column was not
simply replaced by the 1 to its left. Instead, that 1 represents 2d
units of binary numbers just as it would represent 10 units if it
had been written as a decimal number. The two units of 1 are
moved over to where the zero is, and then one is subtracted
from the two *1's*. The result is the correct answer, one.

$$\begin{array}{rcr} 1 \text{ times } 1000 & = & 1000 \\ 0 \text{ times } 100 & = & 0 \\ 1 \text{ times } 10 & = & 10 \\ 0 \text{ times } 1 & = & 0 \\ \hline \text{Total} & = & 1010 \text{ decimal} \end{array}$$

When borrowing in binary, do it just as it would be done in decimal, *except* units of 2 are borrowed instead of units of 10. Now try a more difficult problem:

$$
\begin{array}{cccc}
1 & 0 & 1 & 0 \\
- & 1 & 1 & 1 \\
\hline
\end{array}
$$

Here's how to do it:
    Step 1. Borrow one unit of 2 to replace the right-most zero. As in the first borrowing example, 1b from 10b (2 in decimal) leaves 1b:

$$
\begin{array}{cccc}
 & & & 10 \\
1 & 0 & \cancel{1} & 0 \\
- & 1 & 1 & 1 \\
\hline
 & & & 1 \\
\end{array}
$$

    Step 2. Since there are now two zeros in a row, borrow the one unit of eight to replace the leftmost zero. In essence, the one unit of eight makes two units of 4 in that spot:

$$
\begin{array}{cccc}
 & 2\text{-}4\text{'s} & & \\
\cancel{1} & 0 & \cancel{0} & 0 \\
- & 1 & 1 & 1 \\
\hline
 & & & 1 \\
\end{array}
$$

    Step 3. You can borrow one of those units of four to move one column to the right, and leave one unit of four where it is. One unit of four, or two units of two will be moved:

$$
\begin{array}{cccc}
 & \begin{array}{c}1\text{-}4 \\ 2\text{-}\cancel{4}\text{'s}\end{array} & 2\text{-}2\text{'s} & \\
\cancel{1} & 0 & \cancel{1} & 0 \\
- & 1 & 1 & 1 \\
\hline
 & & & 1 \\
\end{array}
$$

    Step 4. Now the problem can be completed as a simple subtraction problem. One unit of two from the two units of two leaves one unit in the 2's place. Then, one unit of four from one unit of four leaves zero in the 4's place:

$$
\begin{array}{cccc}
 & 1\text{-}4 & & \\
 & 2\text{-}4\text{'s} & 2\text{-}2\text{'s} & \\
\cancel{1} & 0 & \cancel{1} & 0 \\
- & 1 & 1 & 1 \\
\hline
0 & 0 & 1 & 1 \\
\end{array}
$$

$$
\begin{array}{l}
1\ 0\ 1\ 0 \\
-1\ 1\ 1 \\
\hline
0\ 0\ 1\ 1 \\
\end{array}
$$

The answer, then, is 11. To check your answer, add 11 to 111:

$$
\begin{array}{l}
1\ 1\ 1 \\
+1\ 1 \\
\hline
\end{array}
$$

You should get 1010 — if you didn't, check back to the addition portion to see if you missed something. If you did get 1010, and if you have stayed with us to this point, you are ready to move right along.

Two's Complement Subtraction

Inside a real computer the method most commonly used to perform binary subtraction is called *two's complement*. It is more involved than the simple procedure just described but is actually easier for the computer.

Before demonstrating this method, however, some mention should be made of negative numbers. Thus far, only positive numbers have been considered. How does the computer know when a number is positive or negative? Generally it uses a *sign* bit. In an eight bit number, for example, the computer may make one of the bits a 0 when the number is positive and a 1 when it is negative. If your computer uses this method, the sign bit is probably the eighth bit on the left (the most significant bit).

$$\underline{0}1101110$$

↑
sign bit

The number above is positive because there is a 0 in the eighth position. The other seven bits tell us the exact quantity designated by the number. In this case 01101110 binary is +110 decimal. Note that it would be easy to add two binary numbers that are large enough to produce a *carry* into the eighth column where the sign bit is stored. That would cause a condition known as *overflow,* and the answer would be incorrect just as the answer on your pocket calculator would be wrong if the capacity of the display were exceeded. Both computers and calculators have special circuits or instructions to detect overflow and adjust for it.

There is a curious relationship between positive and negative numbers that makes it possible to subtract by *adding.* Consider an example in decimal. Suppose you want to subtract 4 from 8. It is possible to obtain the answer by adding the complement of 4 to the number 8. What's a complement? In decimal it is a number that when added to the number to be complemented, produces the sum of 10 decimal.

The complement of four is six $(4+6=10)$. Now if 6 is added to 8 the result is 14. Drop the 1 in the tens column and 4 is left, the answer to the subtraction problem $(8-4=4)$. This is called the ten's complement system.

With binary numbers the complement of a number is obtained by changing each 1 to a 0 and each 0 to a 1.

1011
0100 (complement of 1011)

This process is called *one's complement.* If the carry is ignored, complementing a binary number is the equivalent of finding the number that can be added to the original number to produce a sum of zero, if a 1 is added to the answer—thus the name *one's complement.*

$$10110$$
$$\underline{+01001} \text{ complement}$$
$$11111$$
$$\underline{+1}$$
$$100000 \text{ zero if carry bit is ignored}$$

Can complementing be used to accomplish binary subtraction by adding as in ten's complement? Here is an example:

Binary	Decimal

$$
\begin{array}{c}
1011 \\
-0010 \\
\hline
\end{array}
\qquad
\begin{array}{c}
11 \\
-2 \\
\hline
9
\end{array}
$$

$$
\begin{array}{l}
1011 \\
+1101 \text{ complement of } 1011 \\
\hline
11000
\end{array}
$$

The answer is 8 if the 1 that was carried over to the fifth column is ignored. That is one less than the correct answer. To obtain the correct answer it is necessary to take the 1 that was carried (also called the overflow) to the fifth row and add it to the answer.

$$
\begin{array}{l}
1011 \\
+1101 \\
\hline
11000 \text{ one's complement} \\
\underline{\quad\text{---}1} \text{ plus overflow} \\
1001 \text{ correct answer}
\end{array}
$$

In a similar process called *two's complement* subtraction, the same thing is accomplished in a slightly different manner. Suppose it is necessary to subtract 1001 from 1110. First find the complement of 1001 which would be 0110. Then add 1 to it to get a sum of 0111. Then add 1001 to 0111. The result is:

$$
\begin{array}{l}
1110 \\
+0111 \\
\hline
10101
\end{array}
\quad \text{same as} \quad
\begin{array}{c}
14 \\
-9 \\
\hline
5
\end{array}
$$

carry bit

In the example above the carry bit is ignored and the binary answer (0101) is the same as the decimal answer (5). The significance of negative numbers in relation to two's complement addition as a way of subtracting is best illustrated by an example using 8 bit numbers with the eight bit indicating whether the number is positive or negative. The binary number 00000011 equals +3 decimal. The two's complement (one's complement +1) is 11111101 which is a negative number since the eighth bit is a 1. This number represents a negative 3. That may be hard to swallow since it certainly doesn't look like a −3. If, indeed, it is a −3 it should be possible to add +3 to it and get 0 as an answer:

$$
\begin{array}{ll}
11111101 & \text{Negative 3} \\
\underline{+1} & \\
11111110 & \text{Negative 2} \\
\underline{+1} & \\
11111111 & \text{Negative 1} \\
\underline{+1} & \\
100000000 &
\end{array}
$$

If the carry bit in the ninth position is discarded, adding +3 does indeed produce 0. Thus, adding the two's complement of a number should be the equivalent of subtraction since we are actually adding the negative of the number. In algebraic terms this relationship is expressed by showing that A-B is the same as A+(−B). Most microcomputers subtract by adding the two's complement of a number.

Binary Multiplication

It is actually easier to multiply in binary than in decimal since there are only two possible results: $1 \times 1 = 1$ while both 0×0, and 0×1 equal 0. Here is an example:

Binary	Decimal
110	6
× 101	× 5
110	
000	
110	
11110	30

In the example, the top number was written down exactly when it was multiplied by a 1 while a row of zeroes was entered when it was multiplied by a zero. Remember to shift each succeeding row over one space to the left just as is done in decimal multiplication. The rows are then added to produce the final answer. One other thing which must be watched carefully in multiplication is the number of ones which are *carried*. An example will illustrate the point:

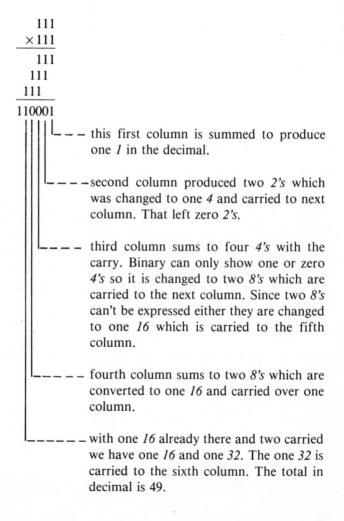

         111
      × 111
         111
         111
      111
      110001

— — — this first column is summed to produce one *1* in the decimal.

— — —second column produced two *2's* which was changed to one *4* and carried to next column. That left zero *2's*.

— — — third column sums to four *4's* with the carry. Binary can only show one or zero *4's* so it is changed to two *8's* which are carried to the next column. Since two *8's* can't be expressed either they are changed to one *16* which is carried to the fifth column.

— — — fourth column sums to two *8's* which are converted to one *16* and carried over one column.

— — — with one *16* already there and two carried we have one *16* and one *32*. The one *32* is carried to the sixth column. The total in decimal is 49.

Binary Division

Again there is a great deal of similarity between division using decimal numbers and division in binary. Consider this example:

```
        10101                    21
111)10010011               7)147
    111                      14
    1000                     07
     111                      7
     111                      0
     111
       0
```

As the example indicates, if you understand binary subtraction you can probably do binary division. If there is a binary remainder it is sometimes signified by an R (e.g., 101 R 1).

It is also possible to make use of a *radix* point and to continue the process of binary division just as is done in decimal division. In the case of binary numbers, however, it is called a binary point, not a decimal point. Just what would the binary digits to the right of a binary point mean? They are the inverse of the number they signify if they occupied the same relative position to the left of the point. The table below should help clarify the relationship:

5	4	3	2	1	.	1	2	3	4	5	Column
2^4	2^3	2^2	2^1	2^0	.	2^{-1}	2^{-2}	2^{-3}	2^{-4}	2^{-5}	Exponential Value
$\frac{16}{1}$	$\frac{8}{1}$	$\frac{4}{1}$	$\frac{2}{1}$	$\frac{1}{1}$	.	$\frac{1}{2}$	$\frac{1}{4}$	$\frac{1}{8}$	$\frac{1}{16}$	$\frac{1}{32}$	Fractional Value in decimal
16	8	4	2	1	.	.5	.25	.125	.0625	.0156	Decimal Value of a binary "1" in that position

Using the table is a convenient way to convert 11.11 binary to decimal:

11 equals, in binary, one "2" and one "1" or 3.

.11 equals, in binary, one ".5" and one ".25" or .75.

The total is thus 3.75 in decimal.

By now you may be thinking "enough is enough — there can't be much more to computer numbers that I need to know." A great deal of the essential information has already been presented. You are much more than half way through. On the other hand, some of the juicy details of binary numbers have not been covered. If you find yourself in need of more information on just how microcomputers do their thing in binary, there are many articles in the computer magazines on the topic. One of the most detailed, though somewhat difficult to follow at times, is Tom Pittman's piece in the October, 1977 issue of ROM. A continuation of that article appeared in the December, 1977 ROM. Pitmann discusses the different ways various computer chips handle the intricacies in computer math and provides as much depth as most people will ever need.

TYPES OF NUMBERS

One topic which has not been considered thus far is the fact that many BASICs (a high level computer language) can represent a number in several different ways, depending on the potential uses of that number and its size. Since most micros use an 8 bit byte, a limit is placed on the size of the number that can be represented. With the full 8 bit byte available a number from 0 to 255 could be represented (e.g. binary 00000000 to binary 11111111). In many business programs, and certainly in statistics programs, the limitation imposed by 8 bit numbers would make meaningful programs impossible. BASICs use a variety of methods to get around the limits of 8 bit numbers. In most cases it will not be necessary for the programmer and computer user to understand just how BASIC does its number juggling act, but it is very important that both the programmer and user have a clear grasp of the end products — the numbers that are used and produced in a BASIC program. Here are some examples of the types of numbers:

Integers

12, 1, − 34, 600000, 436

All the numbers listed above are integer or whole numbers. Some BASICs can only handle integer numbers. Such BASICs are often limited not only to integers but to a specific subset of integer numbers (e.g. only numbers between -65535 and $+65535$). While it may be handy to use only whole or integer numbers in many game and educational programs, a BASIC that understands only integers is too restrictive to be of use in most business and scientific applications.

Single Precision Numbers

123456, 1234.45, .66666, .000001, 963451

All the numbers above are single precision. In most of the BASICs currently in use, single precision means the number will be accurate to six digits. The number 123456 and the number .123456 both have six digits although one is very large while the other equals slightly less than thirteen hundredths. In an actual program the larger number might actually have been 123456.119764. Because the computer using single precision numbers can only deal with 6 significant digits the number was rounded to its 6 most significant digits (e.g. 123456). The number .123456 might have been .1234561211 before it was rounded to its 6 most significant digits.

In many programs single precision numbers will do quite nicely. They provide enough accuracy to produce answers that are close enough to be considered acceptable.

Extended Precision Numbers

In TRS-80 BASIC (the one used by Radio Shack), there is a function (that term will be explained later) which is written like this:

CDBL(X)

If the computer is told to PRINT CDBL(X) it will print the number assigned to the letter X using *double precision*. Many BASICs allow a number to be expressed in an expanded format that includes more significant digits than are allowed in single precision. The Radio Shack computer, for example, includes 16 digits in its double precision numbers:

.123457 single precision

.1234567890123456 double precision

Double precision is accomplished by setting aside extra memory to store the number. Most computers with full size BASICs will permit the use of at least single precision numbers, and many allow double precision numbers; a few even work with triple or larger precision numbers. The number of significant digits used to express a particular number can affect the accuracy of any computations done later in the program. In research, financial, and statistical programs the extra trouble required to use extended precision numbers may be a small price to pay for the greater accuracy that is achieved.

Scientific Notation

On some computers the beginning programmer is likely to encounter a line like this:

$$X = 6.24351E + 09$$

The number above has 6 significant digits, but it also has some extra baggage after those 6 digits. What does the "E + 09" mean? It is a way of indicating very large or very small numbers while still printing only 6 digits on the screen. This method is known as *scientific notation*. The E + 09 is actually an instruction to move the decimal point 9 places to the right to express the number in standard notation:

6.24351E + 09 is the same as 6243510000.

If E − 09 is substituted for E + 09 the decimal point is moved 9 places to the left:

6.24351E − 09 is the same as .00000000624351

Another term used to designate this form of notation is *floating point* since placement of the decimal point is not specified beforehand. Instead it is indicated by the number and sign that follows E. The first part of a number expressed in

scientific notation (e.g. 6.24351) is called the *mantissa* while the part that follows the E is called the *exponent.*
Here are some more examples:

222.111E +03 is the same as 222111.

.143210E +08 is the same as 14321000.

0672.105E −04 is the same as .0672105.

222.111E −09 is the same as .000000222111.

Hexadecimal and Octal Numbers

In the early days, computers were big brutes that insisted on having everything their way. Even very large programs, for example, were written in binary—something few sane people would do today. Binary numbers have one redeeming characteristic—computers understand them. Unfortunately, they are hard to work with, difficult to decode, and messy to display. Early personal computers like the ALTAIR 8800, for example, had over 30 lights on the front panel to display binary numbers. For most of us those lights are more confusing than informative.

Few people actually program directly in binary today. Instead, there are two other number systems, hexadecimal and octal, that stand between the two extremes of computer oriented binary and people oriented decimal. Understanding these two number systems is a major step toward understanding computer programs and languages.

Hexadecimal and octal numbers make machine language programming easier. When hexadecimal or octal numbers are used, the computer still deals with binary numbers. The computer user, however, enters programs and data using the easier to understand hex or octal numbers. The hardware or software in the computer translates the users input into pure binary.

Of the two systems, hex and octal, hex is by far the most popular in personal computing, but it would just be too easy if everyone agreed to use one or the other. If your computer system uses hex, though, it is not necessary to commit to heart the material on octal and vice-versa.

Table 2-2 lists the common number systems, their base, and the symbols available in each system. Most of us learned our adding and subtracting in the decimal system. It uses 10 different values (0 to 9 in this case). If two numbers such as 6 and 7 are to be added, the resulting value cannot be expressed by any of the 10 numerals available. The decimal system uses the concept of *place value* to handle that problem. The symbols or numerals in the first or rightmost position of a whole number have values between 0 and 9. Numerals to the left of that first digit have values that are ten times the value they would have if they were moved one place to the right. Thus 6 plus 7 is expressed in the base ten or decimal system as *1 ten and 3 ones* or 13.

Table 2-2   Number Systems

Name	Base	Symbols
Binary	2	0, 1
Octal	8	0, 1, 2, 3, 4, 5, 6, 7, 8
Decimal	10	0, 1, 2, 3, 4, 5, 6, 7, 8, 9
Hexadecimal	16	0, 1, 2, 3, 4, 5, 6, 7, 8, 9, A, B, C, D, E, F

Now what about octal and hexadecimal numbers? Hex uses sixteen different numerals. From 0 to 9 the numerals are the same in hex as in decimal. After nine in decimal, though, part of the value is *carried* over to the next column on the left. In hex there are six more numerals or symbols (A, B, C, D, E, F) that must be used before a carry operation is performed. Thus 9 plus 1 is 10 in decimal, but it is A in hex. In hex the numeral D, for example, stands for the same number as does decimal 13. The hex numeral 10 (1 *sixteen* and 0 *ones*) equals the decimal value 16 (1 *ten* and 6 *ones*). The important thing to remember about hex numbers is that their place value is a power of 16, not 10. Thus 2 in hex is 2 in decimal: hex 20 is decimal 32 (2 *sixteens*), and 40 hex is 64 decimal (4 *sixteens*). B hex is 11 decimal while B0 is 176 (11 *sixteens*). Tables for converting between hex and decimal can be found in an appendix. Table 2-3 will also help with converting.

The octal system works on the same principle as hex, but instead of 16 different numerals it uses only eight (0-7). Convert-

Table 2-3   Base Conversion Table

BIN	OCT	DEC	HEX	BIN	OCT	DEC	HEX
0	0	0	00	110110	66	54	36
1	1	1	01	110111	67	55	37
10	2	2	02	111000	70	56	38
11	3	3	03	111001	71	57	39
100	4	4	04	111010	72	58	3A
101	5	5	05	111011	73	59	3B
110	6	6	06	111100	74	60	3C
111	7	7	07	111101	75	61	3D
1000	10	8	08	111110	76	62	3E
1001	11	9	09	111111	77	63	3F
1010	12	10	0A	1000000	100	64	40
1011	13	11	0B	1000001	101	65	41
1100	14	12	0C	1000010	102	66	42
1101	15	13	0D	1000011	103	67	43
1110	16	14	0E	1000100	104	68	44
1111	17	15	0F	1000101	105	69	45
10000	20	16	10	100110	106	70	46
10001	21	17	11	100111	107	71	47
10010	22	18	12	1001000	110	72	48
10011	23	19	13	1001001	111	73	49
10100	24	20	14	1001010	112	74	4A
10101	25	21	15	1001011	113	75	4B
10110	26	22	16	1001100	114	76	4C
10111	27	23	17	1001101	115	77	4D
11000	30	24	18	1001110	116	78	4E
11001	31	25	19	1001111	117	79	4F
11010	32	26	1A	1010000	120	80	50
11011	33	27	1B	1010001	121	81	51
11100	34	28	1C	1010010	112	82	52
11101	35	29	1D	1010011	123	83	53
11110	36	30	1E	1010100	124	84	54
11111	37	31	1F	1010101	125	85	55
100000	40	32	20	1010110	126	86	56
100001	41	33	21	1010111	127	87	57
100010	42	34	22	1011000	130	88	58
100011	43	35	23	1011001	131	89	59
100100	44	36	24	1011010	132	90	5A
100101	45	37	25	1011011	133	91	5B
100110	46	38	26	1011100	134	92	5C
100111	47	39	27	1011101	135	93	5D
101000	50	40	28	1011110	136	94	5E
101001	51	41	29	1011111	137	95	5F
101010	52	42	2A	1100000	140	96	60
101011	53	43	2B	1100001	141	97	61
101100	54	44	2C	1100010	142	98	62
101101	55	45	2D	1100011	143	99	63
101110	56	46	2E	1100100	144	100	64
101111	57	47	2F	1100101	145	101	65
110000	60	48	30	1100110	146	102	66
110001	61	49	31	1100111	147	103	67
110010	62	50	32	1101000	150	104	68
110011	63	51	33	1101001	151	105	69
110100	64	52	34	1101010	152	106	6A
110101	65	53	35	1101011	153	107	6B

Nailing Jelly to a Tree

BIN	OCT	DEC	HEX	BIN	OCT	DEC	HEX
1101100	154	108	6C	10100110	246	166	A6
1101101	155	109	6D	10100111	247	167	A7
1101110	156	110	6E	10101000	250	168	A8
1101111	157	111	6F	10101001	251	169	A9
1110000	160	112	70	10101010	252	170	AA
1110001	161	113	71	10101011	253	171	AB
1110010	162	114	72	10101100	254	172	AC
1110011	163	115	73	10101101	255	173	AD
1110100	164	116	74	10101110	256	174	AE
1110101	165	117	75	10101111	257	175	AF
1110110	166	118	76	10110000	260	176	B0
1110111	167	119	77	10110001	261	177	B1
1111000	170	120	78	10110010	262	178	B2
1111001	171	121	79	10110011	263	179	B3
1111010	172	122	7A	10110100	264	180	B4
1111011	173	123	7B	10110101	265	181	B5
1111100	174	124	7C	10110110	266	182	B6
1111101	175	125	7D	10110111	267	183	B7
1111110	176	126	7E	10111000	270	184	B8
1111111	177	127	7F	10111001	271	185	B9
10000000	200	128	80	10111010	272	186	BA
10000001	201	129	81	10111011	273	187	BB
10000010	202	130	82	10111100	274	188	BC
10000011	203	131	83	10111101	275	189	BD
10000100	204	132	84	10111110	276	190	BD
10000101	205	133	85	10111111	277	191	BF
10000110	206	134	86	11000000	300	192	C0
10000111	207	135	87	11000001	301	193	C1
10001000	210	136	88	11000010	302	194	C2
10001001	211	137	89	11000011	303	195	C3
10001010	212	138	8A	11000100	304	196	C4
10001011	213	139	8B	11000101	305	197	C5
10001100	214	140	8C	11000110	306	198	C6
10001101	215	141	8D	11000111	307	199	C7
10001110	216	142	8E	11001000	310	200	C8
10001111	217	143	8F	11001001	311	201	C9
10010000	220	144	90	11001010	312	202	CA
10010001	221	145	91	11001011	313	203	CB
10010010	222	146	92	11001100	314	204	CC
10010011	223	147	93	11001101	315	205	CD
10010100	224	148	94	11001110	316	206	CE
10010101	225	149	95	11001111	317	207	CF
10010110	226	150	96	11010000	320	208	D0
10010111	227	151	97	11010001	321	209	D1
10011000	230	152	98	11010010	322	210	D2
10011001	231	153	99	11010011	323	211	D3
10011010	232	154	9A	11010100	324	212	D4
10011011	223	155	9B	11010101	325	213	D5
10011100	234	156	9C	11010110	326	214	D6
10011101	235	157	9D	11010111	327	215	D7
10011110	236	158	9E	11011000	330	216	D8
10011111	237	159	9F	11011001	331	217	D9
10100000	240	160	A0	11011010	332	218	DA
10100001	241	161	A1	11011011	333	219	DB
10100010	242	162	A2	11011100	334	220	DC
10100011	243	163	A3	11011101	335	221	DD
10100100	244	164	A4	11011110	336	222	DE
10100101	245	165	A5	11011111	337	223	DF

BIN	OCT	DEC	HEX	BIN	OCT	DEC	HEX
11100000	340	224	E0	11110000	360	240	F0
11100001	341	225	E1	11110001	361	241	F1
11100010	342	226	E2	11110010	362	242	F2
11100011	343	227	E3	11110011	363	243	F3
11100100	344	228	E4	11110100	364	244	F4
11100101	345	229	E5	11110101	365	245	F5
11100110	346	230	E6	11110110	366	246	F6
11100111	347	231	E7	11110111	367	247	F7
11101000	350	232	E8	11111000	370	248	F8
11101001	351	233	E9	11111001	371	249	F9
11101010	352	234	EA	11111010	372	250	FA
11101011	353	235	EB	11111011	373	251	FB
11101100	354	236	EC	11111100	374	252	FC
11101101	355	237	ED	11111101	375	253	FD
11101110	356	238	EE	11111110	376	254	FE
11101111	357	239	EF	11111111	377	255	FF

ing a binary number to an octal number requires two steps. First, divide the binary number into groups of three bits beginning on the right. Then write the octal equivalent of the value of each group of three. Here is an example:

Binary   1011101

          010 111 101   Step 1

Octal   2   7   5   Step 2

The first binary group on the right, 101, can be read as *1 four, 0 twos, and 1 one* which adds up to 5 in octal. The two and the seven were derived in the same manner. An extra zero was added to the last group of three to fill out the set.

Converting binary into hexadecimal is a similar process except that the binary number is grouped into sets of four:

Binary 10111101
       1011 1101 Step 1

Hex   B   D   Step 2

In the beginning, however, the easiest way to make these conversions is to look them up in a table. Many computer manuals have conversion tables as appendices.

BOOLEAN ALGEBRA

There are many types or families of concepts in algebra, that mystical branch of higher mathematics that deals primarily with relationships between symbolic representations of values (e.g., $X/2 = Y + B - R/6$). One family, Boolean algebra, is particularly useful to computer designers and programmers because it is based on binary rather than decimal mathematics. There are thus only two numerals, 1 and 0, to be considered; convenient since the computer can only deal with 1's and 0's. Many of the integrated circuits that populate a computer board actually perform some Boolean operation on the signals that pass through them. Let's look at the most common Boolean operations:

AND

In its simplest form AND requires two input signals to produce one output. The input signals can be either 1 or 0, and the output obtained depends on the input pattern. The symbol for an AND function is shown below:

Anytime you see the AND symbol it tells you exactly what to expect at Z if you know what signals are at X and Y. The pattern to be expected is shown in a *truth table* such as the one below:

X	Y	Z
0	0	0
0	1	0
1	0	0
1	1	1

Truth Table for AND Function

The first line of the table says *If both signals X and Y are 0 then the output signal Z will be 0.* In fact, the only way to get a 1 at Z with an AND function is for both X and Y to be 1. Figure 2-3 shows the pinout diagram of the 7408, a very common IC; there

is probably one in your computer. If you ground pin 7 and put 5
volts DC on pin 14 the chip has four independent AND gates.
Pin 11, for example, will be low (0) unless a 1 appears on pins 13
and 12. In this IC, and the others in a family of IC's called TTL
(transistor to transistor logic) a 1 means a positive voltage of
something greater thán 2.4 volts while a logic 0 is less than .8
volts.

   In addition to the hardware AND chips described thus far,
the AND function can be obtained via software. The 8080 and
Z-80 microprocessors have an instruction ANI or *AND Immediate* with the accumulator. The instruction is followed by an
8 bit binary number (the *immediate*) which the computer will
AND with whatever number is stored in the accumulator (a

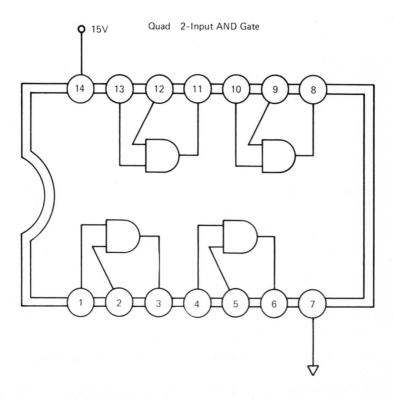

Figure 2-3   Logic diagram for the 7408

register in the computer). Other 8080 instructions allow the programmer to AND the number stored in the accumulator with
the value in any memory location.

Suppose the two bytes below were stored in two memory locations in the computer;

10110100 first byte

00110011 second byte

If an instruction called for the computer to AND the bytes in
the memory locations where these bytes reside, the result will be
obtained by applying the set of rules given below to each pair of
bits:

If both bits are 0, the result is 0.

If both bits are 1, the result is 1.

If one bit is 0 and the other is 1, the result is 0.

Using these rules the result of an AND of our two bytes would
be 00110000.

OR

The OR function is the logical reverse of AND. You only get
a 0 out if X and Y are both 0. Anything else produces a 1. The
truth table and logic symbol are shown below:

X	Y	Z
0	0	0
0	1	1
1	0	1
1	1	1

Truth Table for OR Function   Symbol for OR Function

The OR function can be obtained by using hardware such as
the 7432 integrated circuit whose diagram is shown in Figure 2-4.

XOR

Exclusive OR or XOR is similar to OR as the truth table shows.

X	Y	Z
0	0	0
0	1	1
1	0	1
1	1	0

Truth Table for XOR Function

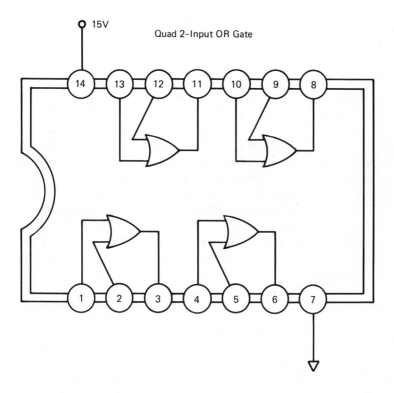

Figure 2-4   Logic diagram of the 7432.

The only difference between OR and XOR occurs when both X and Y are 1. An XOR produces a 0 while an OR produces a 1. XOR *excludes* the *both X and Y at 1* condition from the OR RULES.

NOT, NAND, NOR Functions

There are three additional logic functions which have one thing in common: they invert or reverse the input signals as they are output.

The simplest of these functions is NOT, more commonly called an inverter. The inverter symbol is shown below.

$$X \quad \longrightarrow\!\!\!\!\triangleright\!\circ\!\!-\quad \bar{X}$$

If a 1 appears at the input, a 0 is at the output; a 0 in produces a 1 out. Another word for this function is *complement*. An inverter outputs the complement of its input. The bar over the X at the output indicates it is the *inverse* of X. If $X = 1$, $\bar{X} = 0$ and vice versa. Sometimes in describing signals in the computer, designers will draw a bar over the signal to indicate it is *active low*. For example, suppose you read in your computer manual that the keyboard strobe signal (a brief pulse that is sent each time a key is pressed) is on pin 13 and is normally high. When you press a key the signal will go low for a brief moment. The notation Pin 13 $\overline{STROBE}$ tells you that the signal is active when it is low; a low means a key has been pressed. Had the manual said *Pin 13 STROBE* it would have meant the signal was normally low (0) but went high (1) at each keypress.

The NAND function is a little more complex but still very easy to understand since it is really an *inverted AND* function.

X	Y	Z
1	1	0
1	0	1
0	1	1
0	0	1

$$X \longrightarrow\!\!\!\!\!\!\!\!\rceil\!$$

Truth Table for   **Symbol for NAND Function**
NAND Function

Notice that the logic symbol for NAND is the same as AND with a small circle added at the output. The truth table shows that if we simply invert the output line of AND we get NAND. The 7400 integrated circuit is a commonly used NAND gate.

The relationship between NOR and OR functions is similar to AND and NAND.

X	Y	Z
1	1	0
1	0	0
0	1	0
1	0	1

Truth Table for NOR Function

Symbol for NOR Function

YES

There is one more type of logic function that should be mentioned. The YES function simply takes whatever is at the input and transmits it to the output.

X	Z
0	0
1	1

Truth Table for YES Function   **Symbol for YES Function**

You may wonder why anyone would ever need a logic function that simply outputs what it receives. The fact is YES functions are very popular. They are frequently used to connect two or more sections of electronic equipment that cannot be connected directly. IC's that perform this function are also known as *buffers*. Some computer output lines, for example, can only be connected to one external circuit. You may need to connect those lines to two or more circuits, however, and one way to do that is to connect the computer lines to a buffer IC. The buffer can then be connected to many other circuits.

This is by no means a complete introduction to computer logic but it should be enough to help you figure out what a programmer is trying to do in that program you want to use. Now let's look at the final topic in the chapter—codes.

COMPUTER CODES

It has already been mentioned more times than you ever thought possible in a small book, that inside computers, everything is binary — ones and zeros. Almost everything in the world of humans, however, is alphanumeric — letters and numbers — with decimal numbers being used almost exclusively. The symbols on the computer keyboard are alphanumeric. There must be some orderly way to translate between the symbols we are familiar with and symbols that are computer digestible. The answer is ASCII — American Standard Code for Information Interchange.

When the letter A is pressed on a computer keyboard several things happen. A strobe line sends a brief pulse to the computer to tell it a key has been pressed. The computer then looks at 7 data lines to see what signals are on those lines. In the case of A the lines carry these signals:

	Most Significant Bit					Least Significant Bit
Line Number	7	6	5	4	3	2	1
Signal on Line	1	0	0	0	0	0	1

The ASCII code has a unique 7 bit pattern for all 26 letters, 10 digits, about 30 other symbols such as the bracket, period, comma, and dollar sign, and a set of 32 *control codes*. Control codes are signals that serve some special purpose. CR (0001101) for example, is carriage return. It tells the computer to move the cursor on a video terminal or the printing mechanism on a hardcopy device to the beginning of the line. ASCII is very nearly the universal code in small computers, and it is frequently necessary to decode binary, hex, or octal ASCII to debug or modify machine language (or even BASIC) programs. Table 2-5 is a handy guide to ASCII. The table is printed again in an Appendix so you can tear it out for easier use. Each character's binary, hex, and octal code is printed beside the character. Note that the ASCII binary code in the table has 8 digits rather than 7. The eighth digit is used in some computers as a way of checking for errors. ASCII really needs only 7 bits to define all the characters in the code. The eighth bit is a *parity* bit that is added to each 7 bit byte by the computer as an aid in error checking. With *even parity* the eight bits can always be added together to equal an even number. *Odd parity* produces an odd number. Here is an example.

> 11001001 even parity because there are four 1's
>
> 11001000 odd parity because there are three 1's
>
> 00101000 even parity because there are two 1's
>
> 00101001 odd parity, there are three 1's

When a byte appears with even parity in a system that expects all bytes to have odd parity, an error message may occur. It tells the operator that something is amiss.

There are a few other codes occasionally encountered by the small computer user. The printers that are based on the Selectric typewriter mechanism use one of several non-ASCII codes; older Teletypes may use an outmoded code called BAUDOT, and some manufacturers of computer peripherals have seen fit to use non-standard codes. For the most part, however, ASCII will be your code. Can you decode the hex ASCII code given below?

54 48 55 53 45 4E 44 53

41 4E 4F 54 48 45 52

43 48 41 50 54 45 52 21

Table 2.5 128 Character ASCII Table

Character	Binary—Bit 7 to Bit 0	Octal	Decimal	Hexadecimal
`	01100000	140	096	60
a	01100001	141	097	61
b	01100010	142	098	62
c	01100011	143	099	63
d	01100100	144	100	64
e	01100101	145	101	65
f	01100110	146	102	66
g	01100111	147	103	67
h	01101000	150	104	68

Character	Binary—Bit 7 to Bit 0	Octal	Decimal	Hexadecimal
i	01101001	151	105	69
j	01101010	152	106	6A
k	01101011	153	107	6B
l	01101100	154	108	6C
m	01101101	155	109	6D
n	01101110	156	110	6E
o	01101111	157	111	6F
p	01110000	160	112	70
q	01110001	161	113	71
r	01110010	162	114	72
s	01110011	163	115	73
t	01110100	164	116	74
u	01110101	165	117	75
v	01110110	166	118	76
w	01110111	167	119	77
x	01111000	170	120	78
y	01111001	171	121	79
z	01111010	172	122	7A
{	01111011	173	123	7B
|	01111100	174	124	7C
}	01111101	175	125	7D
~	01111110	176	126	7E
DEL	01111111	177	127	7F
NUL	00000000	000	000	00
SOH	00000001	001	001	01
STX	00000010	002	002	02
ETX	00000011	003	003	03
EOT	00000100	004	004	04
ENQ	00000101	005	005	05
ACK	00000110	006	006	06
BEL	00000111	007	007	07
BS	00001000	010	008	08
HT	00001001	011	009	09
LF	00001010	012	010	0A
VT	00001011	013	011	0B
FF	00001100	014	012	0C
CR	00001101	015	013	0D
SO	00001110	016	014	0E
SI	00001111	017	015	0F
DLE	00010000	020	016	10
DC1	00010001	021	017	11
DC2	00010010	022	018	12
DC3	00010011	023	019	13
DC4	00010100	024	020	14
NAK	00010101	025	021	15
SYN	00010110	026	022	16
ETB	00010111	027	023	17
CAN	00011000	030	024	18
EM	00011001	031	025	19
SUB	00011010	032	026	1A
ESC	00011011	033	027	1B
FS	00011100	034	028	1C

Character	Binary – Bit 7 to Bit 0	Octal	Decimal	Hexadecimal
GS	00011101	035	029	1D
RS	00011110	036	030	1E
US	00011111	037	031	1F
SP	00100000	040	032	20
!	00100001	041	033	21
"	00100010	042	034	22
#	00100011	043	035	23
$	00100100	044	036	24
%	00100101	045	037	25
&	00100110	046	038	26
'	00100111	047	039	27
(	00101000	050	040	28
)	00101001	051	041	29
*	00101010	052	042	2A
+	00101011	053	043	2B
,	00101100	054	044	2C
–	00101101	055	045	2D
.	00101110	056	046	2E
/	00101111	057	047	2F
0	00110000	060	048	30
1	00110001	061	049	31
2	00110010	062	050	32
3	00110011	063	051	33
4	00110100	064	052	34
5	00110101	065	053	35
6	00110110	066	054	36
7	00110111	067	055	37
8	00111000	070	056	38
9	00111001	071	057	39
:	00111010	072	058	3A
;	00111011	073	059	3B
<	00111100	074	060	3C
=	00111101	075	061	3D
>	00111110	076	062	3E
?	00111111	077	063	3F
@	01000000	100	064	40
A	01000001	101	065	41
B	01000010	102	066	42
C	01000011	103	067	43
D	01000100	104	068	44
E	01000101	105	069	45
F	01000110	106	070	46
G	01000111	107	071	47
H	01001000	110	072	48
I	01001001	111	073	49
J	01001010	112	074	4A
K	01001011	113	075	4B
L	01001100	114	076	4C
M	01001101	115	077	4D
N	01001110	116	078	4E
O	01001111	117	079	4F
P	01010000	120	080	50

Character	Binary—Bit 7 to Bit 0	Octal	Decimal	Hexadecimal
Q	01010001	121	081	51
R	01010010	122	082	52
S	01010011	123	083	53
T	01010100	124	084	54
U	01010101	125	085	55
V	01010110	126	086	56
W	01010111	127	087	57
X	01011000	130	088	58
Y	01011001	131	089	59
Z	01011010	132	090	5A
[	01011011	133	091	5B
\	01011100	134	092	5C
]	01011101	135	093	5D
Λ	01011110	136	094	5E
—	01011111	137	095	5F

Abbreviations for Control Characters:

NUL	— null, or all zeros	DC1	— device control 1
SOH	— start of heading	DC2	— device control 2
STX	— start of text	DC3	— device control 3
ETX	— end of text	DC4	— device control 4
EOT	— end of transmission	NAK	— negative acknowledge
ENQ	— enquiry	SYN	— synchronous idle
ACK	— acknowledge	ETB	— end of transmission block
BEL	— bell	CAN	— cancel
BS	— backspace	EM	— end of medium
HT	— horizontal tabulation	SUB	— substitute
LF	— line feed	ESC	— escape
VT	— vertical tabulation	FS	— file separator
FF	— form feed	GS	— group separator
CR	— carriage return	RS	— record separator
SO	— shift out	US	— unit separator
SI	— shift in	SP	— space
DLE	— data link escape	DEL	— delete

Chapter 3

Software I Have
Known and Loved

When a novice small computer user finally figures out the fundamentals of operating his or her system, it is to be expected that a feeling of satisfaction and accomplishment will follow.

The pleasure of early success often fades though, replaced by feelings of confusion and indecisiveness as the user attempts to move beyond the manuals and the software that come with the computer. In any given month the major small computer magazines such as *Byte, Microcomputing, Interface Age, Creative Computing, Personal Computing,* and *80 Computing* will contain articles and ads that hawk nearly 2,000 programs which promise to do a variety of jobs from diagnosing memory problems to keeping payroll records. Selecting and using software is something all of us must do. It is not as easy, however, as ordering new duds from the Sears catalog. The terms, conventions, and traditions of small computer software development and marketing are often confusing, sometimes contradictory and, seemingly always written for the initiated. This chapter will help you understand computer software and terms like DOS, monitor, assembler, applications software, CP/M, and operating system.

STARTING OPTIONS

Any small computer you're likely to buy will have one of two popular software arrangements. The most common arrangement today involves permanently installing a high level language such as BASIC in the computer's ROM or Read Only Memory. Computers such as the TRS-80, Apple II, PET, Texas Instru-

ments, Atari, and Exidy Sorcerer all have BASIC in ROM.
When the computer is switched on it automatically prepares itself to write or run programs written in BASIC, a *high level*
language. What is a high level language? There are actually
three levels of computer language, each with major advantages
and disadvantages. There are machine languages, assembly languages, and higher level languages. Higher level computer languages like BASIC use English-like words in their vocabulary
and accept decimal numbers. A 12 is a 12, nothing else. Whereas
machine and assembly languages are written specifically for a
particular computer, higher level languages are written for a
particular purpose. FORTRAN (FORmula TRANslator), for
example, is the language most used by universities and scien-
tists; COBOL (COmmon Business Oriented Language) is a
popular business language, and BASIC (Beginners All Purpose
Symbolic Instruction Code) is the best known language for
general purpose programming with small computers.

Although the most popular languages have been mentioned
already there are many others. Some of them are used in
specialized applications. LISP was written for work in artificial
intelligence; PILOT is a language for writing computer assisted
instruction. Other languages have small but vocal groups of
devotees who firmly believe their favorite language has the
features needed to make it the best choice for one or more areas
of application.

Thus far only three languages, BASIC, PASCAL, and FOR-
TRAN, are generally available for use on personal computers.
FOCAL (Formulating On-Line Calculations in Algebraic Language) is supported by some micro systems but has generated
less interest than the others. FORTRAN, too, is running far
behind BASIC in popularity. PASCAL is running hard to catch
up, but for the time being BASIC is close to being the universal
language of personal computing. Most of the programs available in magazines are written in it, and computer stores generally stock numerous books that contain the listings of hundreds of
programs written in BASIC.

All the computers mentioned earlier *speak* BASIC as soon as
they are switched on. This feature is a convenience that is provided with more and more of the new models.

Computers that speak BASIC are easier to program than

those that understand only machine or assembly language, and programs written in BASIC can often be transferred form one computer to another. That means someone, somewhere in the world, has probably written a BASIC program to do exactly what you have in mind.

There is one fly in the BASIC ointment, however, which creates a major problem for beginners. Although languages like FORTRAN and COBOL are now fairly standardized thanks to the work of ANSI (American National Standards Institute), the ANSI standard for BASIC are relatively new, and many versions for small computers were written before the standard was established. That means a program written for the BASIC that is used in Apple computers may not run in the BASIC used by the TRS-80 or the PET.

There are also several levels of BASIC on the market. They range from Tiny BASIC, a miniscule language that takes up less than 2K (K stands for 1024) of memory and has a very small vocabulary, to Extended BASIC which has a large and sophisticated vocabulary and requires 16K of memory. Programs which are not written in the version you are using may require extensive modification before they work, or they may not run at all. Everything considered, however, we would urge you to learn at least one version of BASIC and to take advantage of the thousands of free or inexpensive programs that are available today.

All the higher level languages were written with a human user in mind. A programmer can look at the listing of a program and understand what is supposed to happen with each instruction. In BASIC, for example, if you want to have the computer add two values, say A and B, and print the results, the instruction would look something like this:

PRINT A + B

If A and B have not previously been given a value the program would be a little longer:

LET A = 4

LET B = 6

PRINT A + B

Even individuals who have no knowledge of BASIC can understand the meaning of simple programs. Compared to writing programs in machine or assembly language, programming in a higher language is like writing a letter home to mother.

A program written in BASIC or some other high level language is first translated into machine language before it is run on a computer. The program that does the translating takes each of the statements written in the high level language and converts it into machine language instructions. One BASIC statement may require a long series of machine language instructions to replace it when the translation is made.

Translation is handled by two types of programs: compilers and interpreters. A BASIC compiler will take a program written in BASIC and completely translate the program into machine language. It may then be run immediately or saved and run later. Once the translation is done the first time, it need not be translated again (assuming the machine language version is saved).

A BASIC interpreter is the software stored in ROM in the TRS-80, the Apple, PET and many other computers. An interpreter translates the program piece by piece. It also runs the program at the same time. That is, it translates enough to know what to do first, does that, then translates a little more, does that, and so on. (At present almost all microcomputers use interpreters rather than compilers for translation).

Interpreters require less memory than compilers and they are easier to develop initially. They also provide the programmer with more control than compilers. Mistakes generally produce error messages that identify the problem and aid the programmer in debugging the program without having to compile it each time a correction is made. Interpreters, however, are much slower and they require the computer to translate the program every time it is run. And if a particular set of instructions or a subroutine is used over and over in a program, a compiler would only translate the subroutine once while an interpreter would do it every time the subroutine was used.

Programs written in higher level languages take more memory than machine or assembly langauge programs, and they run slower regardless of the method used for translation. They do have two major advantages that make them the most popular means of writing software. The first is that they are easy to understand and learn. In one afternoon it is possible to learn enough BASIC to write your own simple programs. The second reason for their popularity is the fact that they are less dependent on the machine being used. A FORTRAN program written for one computer can be transferred with little difficulty to a computer manufactured by someone else. With BASIC there are likely to be some problems in transferring programs from one version to another, but the difficulties are still far less than those involved in converting a program written in 8080 machine language to the machine language of the 6800 microprocessor.

ROM storage is not the only way to get BASIC into a small computer. Many of the early small systems put the BASIC interpreter software on a cassette tape, a disk, or even on paper tape. Cromemco, Dynabyte, Southwest Technical Products, Heath, and North Star computers all use tape or disk storage for BASIC. When the computer is switched on it cannot understand BASIC. Instead it is under the control of its *operating system* software or the system *monitor* software. A monitor, in the context of software, is a short program, usually stored in ROM, that gives the computer enough *smarts* to load, enter, and/or run other programs.

Each computer will have its own monitor or operating system software which means there is very little standardization. We'll take a look at some typical monitor or operating system later in this chapter. It will help explain just what they do.

SOME TYPICAL MONITOR AND OPERATING SYSTEM SOFTWARE

SOLOS

Although Processor Technology Corporation is no longer in business, their software gained wide acceptance in the industry. It is used by thousands of programmers today both in Sol computers and, with some adaptation, in many other systems. SOLOS is the operating system written for the Sol user. It is a 2048 byte program that makes the separate parts of the computer work together harmoniously.

A computer with SOLOS will usually use a standard ASCII keyboard for input and a CRT (cathode ray tube) video display for output. It may also have a printer for output as well.

When the computer is switched on, its internal wiring causes it to jump to the area of memory where SOLOS is stored and the SOLOS program is executed. First, it places a > on the screen. The > is a *prompt* character that tells you SOLOS has taken control of the computer and is awaiting your instructions. Any instruction given to SOLOS will be in the form of a two letter command followed by any additional information needed to carry out the command. SOLOS will execute a command as soon as the carriage return key (CR) is pressed. Pressing CR signals that the operator is ready for SOLOS to act upon the command. The following sections discuss major commands the SOLOS monitor software understands.

Set Commands

SET S = #hex

When this command is typed in, SOLOS adjusts the speed of the video display. SOLOS automatically sets the default display speed at 0, the fastest rate, but it can be changed with this command. The number after the equal sign can be any hexadecimal number between 0 and FF. *SET* S = FF will cause material being displayed on the screen to appear very slowly. There will actually be a pause between the appearance of each letter. Usually a programmer will want the display to operate at maximum speed, but there are some occasions which call for slower speeds (e.g., displaying the contents of the computer's memory in order to find a particular code or when a game program calls for the display to slowly reveal information or graphics on the screen.) Once a SET S = #h instruction is executed SOLOS will continue to use the display speed selected until another SET S instruction is given, or the computer is switched off or restarted again. *Restart* simply means the computer is instructed to go back to the beginning of SOLOS and start over. Pressing the CONTROL and C keys on many computers causes a restart. When that happens SOLOS erases all the instructions it has received and sets everything to their *default* values.

Note that the SE in SET is underlined. That is because SOLOS uses SE as a shorthand for SET. Almost all of the instructions SOLOS understands have a two letter shorthand code.

S͟E͟T I = #

S͟E͟T O = #

These two commands allow the programmer to tell SOLOS where to send output to, and where to receive data or input from. SOLOS recognizes the following I/O ports:

0 = video display for output, keyboard for input

1 = Serial port

2 = Parallel port

3 = a port which can be defined by the programmer

The default value for both input and output is 0, or the video display for output and keyboard for input. If *S͟E͟T O = 1* is typed, the computer stops displaying output on the screen and instead sends it to the *serial port*. A *port* is just a place where peripherals such as printers, telephone modems, and sensors can be connected to the computer. A Teletype printer, for example, must be connected to the computer via a serial port. S͟E͟T O = 1 might thus be used to tell the computer to send any output to a Teletype printer which is plugged into the serial connector at the back of the computer.

Now what if you type in the instruction S͟E͟T I = 1? That would tell SOLOS to stop looking to the keyboard for input and look instead to the serial port. If the Teletype is still connected to the computer it will now be necessary to use its keyboard to send SOLOS further instructions — the computer will not respond to its own keyboard anymore.

S͟E͟T N = #

This instruction is an interesting one. Many slow printers, especially Teletype 33's, cannot perform a carriage return quickly. Thus after an ASCII carriage return code is received the printer may still be in the process of moving the print head over to the left margin, (especially when a long line has just been printed and the print head is over on the far right) when the next character to be printed arrives. The result can be missing characters or characters that should be printed on the left margin appearing as strikeovers somewhere else on the line because they were printed as the printhead was moving to left margin. *SET N = 5* tells SOLOS to send five *nulls* to the printer right after every carriage return code. Since an ASCII null (00hex) is interpreted as a *do nothing* code by the printer, the only effect is to give the printer enough extra time to get over to the left margin. Even the slowest printers should be able to perform a carriage return while 5 nulls are being sent, and most need only one (SET N = 1) or two (SET N = 2). The default valve is 0 or no nulls.

SET TAPE = 0 or 1

There are many methods for storing data on cassette tapes, but two of the most popular are the so called *Byte standard* which stores data at the slow rate of 300 BAUD or 300 bits per second, and the CUTS (Computer Users Tape System) 1200 BAUD method from Processor Technology. SE TA = 0 tells SOLOS to conduct all tape operations in the faster CUTS format while SE TA = 1 indicates the slower, and more dependable, Byte format is to be used. The default value is 0 or CUTS.

SET CIN ####hex

SET COUT ####hex

SOLOS has built-in software to handle input and output from a serial port, a paralled port, a keyboard, and a video display. There is, however, an occasional need for special I/O routines written in machine language. These two commands tell SOLOS where *custom input* or *custom output* routines are stored in memory. The number on the right of the equal sign is the starting address, in hex, of the Input or Output routine. If a SET O = 3 is typed, SOLOS will go to the RAM address specified by SE CO = # and execute the instructions stored there each time a character is to be output.

The ESCON conversion system for Selectric typewriters, for example, uses a special output routine to operate the Selectric as a printer. The SET O = 3 command makes it very easy to use ESCON's routines.

SET CRC = FF

Under normal circumstances SOLOS will carefully check the data that is input from cassette tapes. If it finds anything amiss SOLOS stops processing data from the tape and prints out an error message. SET CRC = FF tells SOLOS to forget errors and accept whatever is on the tape. It is handy when there is a minor problem with a tape, but you want to load it into the computer anyway.

Tape Commands

GET

SAVE

SOLOS assumes the mass storage device connected to the computer is a cassette tape recorder. SOLOS allows up to two recorders to be used which are designated Unit 1 and Unit 2. Here is a typical tape command.

GET BASIC/2

The command above tells SOLOS to turn on the motor on recorder number 2 and to look for a program that is named BASIC. If the /2 is omitted SOLOS assumes BASIC is on Unit 1 and will try to read it from there (GET BASIC).

When a GET command is entered, SOLOS begins reading the data on the tape. When it finds a program that has the name specified by the GET command it loads the program into the computer's memory. When that task is completed it prints a message on the screen that tells you it has loaded the program into RAM beginning at a particlar memory address. It also tells the user how long (in bytes) the program is.

The SAVE command works in a similar manner. Suppose you've written a program yourself and now want to store it on tape so that it can be read back into the computer later. It is necessary to give the program a name. SOLOS allows names that are five or less characters long (e.g., MYPRO but not MYPROG). The place where the program begins and ends in memory must also be known.

SAVE MYPRO 0 01AE

The command above tells SOLOS to save the material stored in memory from 0 to 1AE hex on tape and to give it the name MYPRO. Later, if the cassette with MYPRO were read back into memory (GET MYPRO) the data would automatically be placed in memory from 0 to 1AE hex.

CAT

This is a handy command that can get you off the hook when there are five identical cassettes on your desk, one of which has the program you need on it. (Forgot to write the program name on the cassette, didn't you?) CAT will simply list the name of each program, or file, it finds stored on a tape. It is also useful in finding the starting point of a particular program on a tape that has many programs on it. CAT reads the tape and lists the names as they appear on the tape. It also lists the starting address of the program and the total number of bytes occupied.

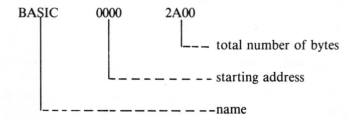

Operating Commands

EXECUTE #H

Once a program is loaded into memory using the GET command, it can be run by typing EX followed by the starting address of the program in hex. EX 0 would instruct the computer to begin following the instructions that are stored in memory location 0 and above. Another command which is abbreviated XEQ, is a combination of GET and EXECUTE. *XEQ BASIC* tells SOLOS to find a program called BASIC on tape, load it into memory, and then execute (RUN) it.

ENTER

DUMP

This pair of commands is used in machine language program-

ming. EN 00FF lets SOLOS know you want to begin entering
data into memory starting at location FF hex. SOLOS then expects to see two digit hexadecimal numbers (e.g., AE) separated
by a space:

10 AE DF 06 08

It will place the first number (in this case, 10) in the memory
location specified after ENTER (e.g., FF hex). The next number
is placed in the next memory location (e.g., 100 hex) and so on.
To terminate ENTER, the programmer types a slash (/) and
presses carriage return. To display whatever is in memory, the
command DUMP is used, DU FF 1FF will cause the data stored
from FF hex to 1FF hex to be displayed on the screen. Although
the data in memory is in binary form SOLOS converts it to
hexadecimal for display.

TERM

The final SOLOS command to be discussed provides a convenient way of using the computer as a *dumb* terminal. TE causes
SOLOS to set up the computer so that it simply transmits and
receives data from another computer. This can be accomplished
by connecting a modem to the serial port. The modem is then
connected to a mainframe computer by telephone.

EXIDY SORCERER Monitor

Processor Technology lives now only in the teary eyes of its
former customers (and perhaps between the lines of all the legal
briefs filed on its demise). Although it is only a guess, it's a good
bet that the arrival of the Exidy Sorcerer computer helped to
usher PT and its venerable SOL computer into that great silicon
gulch in the sky. Sorcerer offered a computer with all of SOL's
features, plus an improved, more modern design for about half
the price ($895 versus around $1900). The Sorcerer is, in fact, so
similar in function and design to the SOL that one is tempted to
wonder aloud whether the gnomes at Exidy didn't sneak more
than one look over the fence at PT before hiking off to
computerland.

The Sorcerer monitor software is very similar to SOLOS but
with some important improvements. Here is a summary of the
Exidy monitor commands:

SET S = #

Same as in SOLOS: sets speed of video display. # can be any number from 0 (fast) to 99 (very slow).

SET O =

SET I =

Defines the current or active I/O ports. A letter after the equal sign designates the particular port to be used. V is for video, K for Keyboard, P for parallel port, L for the serial port (generally used to connect a line printer — thus the L), and S for tape. The Sorcerer will also accept a memory address (e.g., SET O = 1000) where special input or output routines are stored.

DUMP

ENTER

Works just like SOLOS.

SAVE

LOAD

Work much like SAVE and GET in SOLOS.

LOG

Same as EXECUTE in SOLOS.

MOVE # # #

Can be used to transfer data from one section of memory to another. *MOVE 0 500 1000* is an instruction to move the data stored between memory addresses 0 and 500 to another area of memory which begins at 1000. All numbers are decimal.

TE # #

This command performs a comprehensive memory test. It is a very handy feature that every system should have. Each byte of memory is tested, bit by bit. The first number specifies the beginning address of memory to be tested; the second number is the last byte to be tested.

PROMPT =

The Sorcerer will display a > on the screen whenever it is under the control of its monitor software. If > doesn't turn you on as much as * just type in *PR* = * and you have a new prompt character for the monitor.

PP

If a SOL user wanted to use BASIC it was necessary to load the interpreter in from tape. The SORCERER comes with a standard BASIC in a removable ROM pack. When it is inserted in the side of the computer, SORCERER automatically prepares to run BASIC. If the ROM pack is removed or if the command BYE is typed the Sorcerer jumps to its monitor software. When you want to return to BASIC (or any other software in a ROM pack) just type PP.

TRS-80 Monitor

Since Radio Shack's little TRS-80 appeared a few years ago it has been adopted in nearly 250,000 homes, schools, factories, and businesses. There are more TRS-80's out there than any other model, and the trend is still up for Tandy Corporation, the parent company of Radio Shack. Tandy has more engineers who sit by the phone in Fort Worth and answer questions (they have a toll free number) than some manufacturers have on their entire payroll.

With all that success and support you would expect the TRS-80 to have some kind of monitor software. Nothing could be further from the truth. The TRS-80 is aimed at a segment of the market that is interested primarily in BASIC (Tandy's Level II BASIC is one of the best), and strong monitor software is most useful for programmers who work in machine or assembly language. In its standard form it is not possible to use the TRS-80 to write machine language programs. When switched on, it automatically jumps to a BASIC interpreter which is stored in ROM. If the command SYSTEM is typed while the computer is running BASIC, the TRS-80 will jump to its *monitor* or system software which only has two commands that tell the TRS-80 to load and/or run machine language program.

T-BUG

The TRS-80 may not come with a special set of non-BASIC instructions, but there are a number of remedies. One is

T-BUG, a 1K monitor program sold on cassette by Radio Shack for $14.95. When T-BUG is loaded a # appears as the prompt character instead of the familiar READY from BASIC. T-BUG now awaits your command. In a 1K monitor you don't get the champaign supper but it is inexpensive, and better than no monitor at all. Here are its commands.

M####H

Causes the data stored in the memory location specified by the hex number to be displayed on the screen. If you want to change the contents of that memory location it is only necessary to type in the new number. T-BUG puts it in memory and then moves on to the next higher memory location where the same process can be repeated. A location can be skipped by pressing the ENTER key, while pressing X will abort the M command altogether.

R

Causes the contents of all the temporary storage locations (registers) in the Z-80 microprocessor that is the heart (or brains) of the computer to be displayed.

P ####H1 ###H2

P instructs the computer to write the contents of memory (from ####1 to ####2) onto a cassette tape.

L

Loads a program from tape into memory.

B ####H

This command is useful primarily in machine language programming. It sets a *breakpoint*. Whenever the computer reaches the memory location designated by the hex number after B it will jump back to the monitor software and wait for another command. (For a more extensive look at T-BUG, try *Introduction to T-BUG,* by Don and Kurt Inman, available from dilithium Press.)

Rod Hallen's Monitor

Another piece of software that gives the TRS-80 a more powerful monitor was described by Rod Hallen in an article in the April 1979 issue of *Microcomputing*. The program is free if you get the magazine. The entire program takes up about 2K, and is written in BASIC. That means a user can type it in and use the RUN command in TRS-80 BASIC to get it going. Hallen owned a SOL before his Radio Shack computer and the similarity between his monitor and SOLOS is very clear. The commands are:

DUMP

ENTER

EXECUTE

SAVE

LOAD

All five commands above work much as they do in SOLOS.

NORTHSTAR DOS

In the beginning phases of the small computer movement a little known company called Northstar Computers made its mark by selling a high quality, low cost, disk system for computers made by someone else. The Northstar disk, now improved and updated, is still on the market and still selling well. Northstar now markets several pieces of hardware including a well received computer dubbed the Horizon.

One of the things that made the little disk system so popular was the excellent software that comes with it. There is a very good BASIC, interpreters for other languages, including PASCAL, and thousands of dollars worth of educational, business, and game software that will run on computers that have the Northstar disk. The applications software does not come with the system, and very little of it is actually sold by Northstar, but the company does have a regularly published newsletter in which it lists and describes most of the software available for Northstar.

The software that is of interest to us in this section is the DOS or disk operating system and the monitor that comes with each disk.

The Northstar disk system, like most similar systems, comes in two parts, the disk drive itself and a *control board* that contains the circuits required to interface the disk to the computer.

On the control board is a small section of read only memory where a short program resides. It has just enough computing power to load the DOS program into the computer from a disk supplied by Northstar.

A DOS does many of the same jobs in a disk system that a monitor does in a tape based system. The commands in the NS DOS will be discussed first. Another piece of NS software which is actually called a monitor will also be covered briefly.

When the disk system is powered up the DOS is transfered into the computer's memory and a * appears on the screen indicating the computer is now under the control of the DOS. Here are some DOS commands and their meaning:

LIST

Lists the names of all the files on the disk as well as several other pieces of information about each file such as the size of the file, where it is located on the disk, and where it will be placed in memory when loaded.

GO NAME

Typing GO BASIC causes the DOS to load BASIC into memory and then turn control over to the BASIC interpreter; the monitor commands will no longer be understood. GO followed by the name of a file which contains a program will cause that program to be loaded and run.

LF NAME

LF is short for *load file.* It works just like GO except the file named is only loaded into memory. It is not executed as it is with GO.

JP #### hex

JP stands for *jump.* This command will cause the computer

to go to the specified memory address and execute the program located there.

CR NAME

CR is short for *create*. CR MYPROG 10 tells the DOS to put the file name MYPROG in the file directory of the disk and to set aside ten, 256 byte blocks on the disk to store MYPROG. The directory is a sort of roadmap of the disk. It tells what is on the disk, how big it is in terms of blocks (a block is 256 bytes of space) and where each file is located on the disk. A file must be created before it can be used.

DE NAME

DE MYPROG will delete MYPROG from the file directory so you can put something else in that space on the disk.

CO

After a hard day of creating and deleting, the disks you're using will be a little ragged. Programs may be spread all across the disk with many blocks or sections on the disk blank because files have been deleted. CO instructs DOS to go through the disk and compact or tidy up the disk. When it finishes the disk will have all the programs stored on the disk gathered together while all the unoccupied space is placed together making it more usable.

SF NAME

SF saves a section of RAM on disk under the name given after SF.

CF Name1 Name2

CF means *copy file*. It allows the user to copy the file designated by the first name after CF to the file designated by the second name.

CD #1 #2

CD is similar to CF except the entire disk is copied. To use CD (copy disk) it is necessary to have two drives (generally designated 1 and 2). CD 2 1 means *copy the contents of the disk in drive 2 onto the disk which is in drive 1.*

RD #1 #2 #3

WR #1 #2 #3

RD (read disk) and WR (write disk) are used to transfer data between the disk and the system memory. The first number tells DOS the starting block on the disk, the second number is the starting memory address (in hex), and the third number is the number of blocks to be transferred. The disk is arranged into 350 blocks, numbered from 0 to 349. RD 222 1000 10 means *"transfer the data stored in blocks 222 through 232 on the disk (a total of 2560 bytes) into memory beginning at address 1000 hex."*

IN

New disks must be prepared or initialized before they can be used in an NS system. IN causes a disk to be initialized.

DT

Occasionally a disk will behave erratically, either because the program on the disk has an error on it or because the disk itself is damaged. Disks are sensitive to magnetic fields, dust, fingerprints, and humidity. DT tests the entire disk to determine if it is useable.

In addition to a DOS, Northstar also supplies a monitor that has several useful commands. Without going into exactly how each command works, here is a brief description of the more important monitor commands:

CM

Compares data stored in one area of memory with that stored elsewhere.

FM

Used to fill a section of memory with a particular ASCII code.

MM

Moves data stored in one section of memory to another memory location.

SM

Searches memory for a particular code.

TM

Tests the computer memory to determine if it is working properly.

DH and DA

Displays hexadecimal or ASCII codes.

JP

Works same as in DOS.

OS

Causes computer to jump back to the DOS.

OD

Specifies the output device to be used (e.g., CRT, printer)

ID

Specifies the input device to be used (e.g., keyboard, Teletype).

CP/M™*

CP/M, sold by Digital Research, Inc. of Pacific Grove, California, is very different from the software discussed thus far. For one thing it isn't written for any particular system. There are versions currently available for most of the popular small computers.

---

*CP/M is a registered trademark of Digital Research, Inc.

CP/M is also different in that it carries a substantial cost. It sells for $100 direct from Digital Research, and a version for the TRS-80 is priced at $150 from FMG Corporation. Lifeboat Associates of New York offers versions for many computers. Their price is $145.

While large corporations are accustomed to spending hundreds or thousands of dollars on software, small computer users have come to expect quite a bit for software in the *above $100* category. They get it in CP/M. It is a major piece of software that not only provides the user with an expanded, more powerful operating system, it also serves as the foundation for many other programs. Language processors for BASIC, FORTRAN, and COBOL as well as application programs like word processors, data bases, and payroll software have been written for CP/M. These programs use the general purpose software routines incorporated in CP/M to reduce the amount of work that must be done to get a program written, debugged, and on the market. Tailoring applications software to CP/M rather than a particular computer also expands the population of potential purchasers. To the user, having CP/M means being less dependent on the manufacturer of the computer for applications software since most programs written for CP/M can be run on any computer that has CP/M.

CP/M requires a disk system and a substantial amount of memory to be used most effectively. CP/M is thus not part of a typical small system for home use, but an increasing number of businesses are buying disk based systems and CP/M. Such a combination, while priced well above the cost of entry level systems, is very competitive with the minicomputer alternatives that do the same jobs in a business environment. The manuals for CP/M are several hundred pages long, one indication of the reason CP/M will be described only in general here. CP/M is composed of several subcomponents that do a particular job:

Console Command Processor

CCP is part of the real world interface for the system. It is what the user talks to, and it in turn directs some of the activities of other subcomponents. CCP also has built-in routines to handle input and output from peripherals like printers and a CRT.

Basic Disk Operating System

BDOS handles the work of creating files on disks and of transferring data to and from disk storage. BDOS is a very sophisticated piece of software.

Editor

ED is used to create and modify a variety of files. The commands used by ED are a little difficult to learn. For example, + 5D means *delete the next five characters,* + 5C means *move the cursor over five characters without changing anything,* and + 5K means kill or delete the next five lines. Once the codes for the commands are learned, however, the editor is a very powerful tool that can be used in writing and editing programs and text.

Peripheral Interface Program

PIP performs several jobs that are often grouped under the term *utility.* In general the term refers to relatively routine, unglamorous, but necessary, jobs. In CPM the utility work is shared somewhat by PIP and CCP. PIP does some of the input/output management and it also makes it possible to rearrange already existing files. Many programmers use a modular approach which involves breaking a large program into several logically related subroutines. That approach is made easier by PIP which can take several small files containing subroutines and combine them into a large single file.

Dynamic Debugging Tool

DDT is actually a powerful tool for writing and debugging assembly language programs. Assembly language will be covered in a later chapter. CP/M contains an assembler that can be used to write and run programs written in 8080 assembly language as well as a very good BASIC interpreter. CP/M is quite a package.

Troubleshooting Programs and Operating Aids

There are ads in any of the computer magazines for many different types of software designed to meet a particular need on the part of the computer user. It is not possible to cover all of them in detail. Instead a few in some of the major categories will be discussed. Since there are more TRS-80's in use, and thus more software for that computer, the focus will be on TRS-80 compatible software.

Memory Test Programs

A few systems automatically test the memory each time the computer is switched on. Others have a specific monitor or operating system command the programmer can use to test all or part of the memory.

There is good reason to incorporate memory tests in monitor software. RAM is the most problem prone part of many computers and a memory problem is not always easy to diagnose. It may come and go, or cause problems under some circumstances but not others. Several memory test programs are available. One, *RAM Test for Level II,* is available from Mumford Micro in Summerland, California for $9.95. It will conduct a comprehensive test of all the RAM in a TRS-80 in less than 14 seconds.

Cassette Aids

Computers vary in the way they handle loading programs from cassette tape, and the degree of success obtained also varies quite a bit. In some early systems it was almost impossible to successfully load programs from tape.

The probability of success has increased in the newest crop of small computers but there is still room for improvement in many systems. The TRS-80 is a case in point. Its cassette data storage sytem is one of the main reasons some people refer to it as the *trash-80.* That title is probably undeserved, but there is no denying that the TRS-80 cassette system is less dependable than some of its competitors. For $39.95 the DATA/PRINT folks in Fargo, South Dakota promise to deliver you from the perils of unloadable cassettes. Their TRcopy program, when loaded into a TRS-80, promises to work wonders on all those unkept and dirty bits you're trying to load or save on tape. TRcopy improves the cassette system in several ways. Its most interesting feature is its ability to print on the screen the data that is being read from the tape. The user actually sees what's going into memory as the tape is loaded. TRcopy also has facilities for verifying tapes. This means you can check to see if what is on the tape matches what's in memory.

Keyboard Debounce Programs

One annoying habit of the TRS-80 is a tendency to occasionally produce two letters when a key is pressed. Expensive keyboards have special circuits to take care of keybounce — press a key once and you get one character — always. Alas, the TRS-80 is simplicity itself, and it works fine — most of the time. Occasionally, though, you type in PRINT and on the screen you see PRIINT. The TRS-80 Software Exchange sells a $25.00 program that cures keybounce on the TRS-80, makes changing between upper and lower case easier (the TRS-80 is set to print upper case letters unless the shift key is pressed, just the opposite of typewriters) and allows use of the TRS-80 as a terminal.

Terminal Programs

In addition to the terminal program just mentioned, there are several others offered by various vendors that allow the TRS-80 to be used as a remote input device for a large computer. The TRS-80 Software Exchange offers *Smart Terminal* for $50. Hayes Data Systems of Atlanta has TELCOM, a similar program, for $25, and Radio Shack sells a $30 program. These vary in terms of the features they offer and their mode of operation. Be sure the one you buy will do what you want.

Printer Software

Sooner or later almost every computer owner feels the need for *hard copy*. The lucky ones can add a suitable printer to their system easily, perhaps by connecting it in to the proper plug on the back of the computer.

Computers like the TRS-80, however, do not come with the necessary hardware and/or software to run many of the printers on the market today. Small System Software's *TRS232 Printer Interface* permits a standard printer to be interfaced with the computer. The $50 price tag includes all the hardware and software needed to connect a variety of serial printers to the TRS-80.

High Level Language Interpreters

At least one interpreter, usually BASIC, comes with almost every computer sold today. A significant segment of the software market, however, is in the sale of "souped up" or improved versions of BASIC and entirely new interpreters for other languages like FORTRAN, PILOT, COBOL, PASCAL, Tiny C, and LISP. It reminds me of my teenage years. Much of our lunchroom conversation centered around how much extra power could be obtained from a particular short block Chevy V8 if a 4-barrel carb, a quarter race cam and a new set of high compression pistons were installed. Of course, none of us had a short block Chevy V8 to do all that to.

Perhaps it is a human, or at least an American, trait to try and improve on what is. That is just what several companies have done with the BASIC interpreters in today's small computers. GRT Corporation, now defunct, was one of the first to offer enhanced and expanded BASIC interpreters for the TRS-80 and several other computers. Microsoft, the software development company that wrote the BASICs in many small computers, also sells a more powerful BASIC that can be used in the most popular computers.

There are two approaches to adding more features to a BASIC interpreter. The most economical approach involves writing software that is added to the existing interpreter. This approach is particularly sensible when the original interpreter is ROM based, rather than being loaded into RAM from cassette. BASICs in ROM will occupy memory space regardless of whether they are being used or not (unless they're in removable ROM packs) and thus should be used whenever possible. Generally, enhancement software will add features to the original software that are especially useful or convenient. A typical price for one of the enhancement packages is around $50. Is it worth it? Only the user can say. Many people will be able to get along quite nicely with the software that comes with their computer. Others will quickly see the need for more powerful features.

The availability of several interpreters for CP/M based systems has already been mentioned. Many software houses sell a variety of computer languages. They range in price from less than $10 for Tom Pittman's Tiny BASIC for the KIM to well over $500 for a full blown, disk based FORTRAN compiler.

What are some reasons to buy an interpreter or a compiler? One major reason is the need for a language with more sophisticated or convenient instructions. The BASIC instruction

PRINT, for example, is available in every BASIC interpreter. PRINT, in its plain vanilla form, is an instruction to print out whatever follows on the line. The enhanced BASIC's usually have several variations of PRINT that can be used in special circumstances (see PRINT USING in Chapter 9 for examples).

Another reason to buy an extra high level language interpreter is the flexibility it provides. I own six different BASIC interpreters for my SOL systems. If I find a particular piece of software written in a dialect of BASIC that is not compatible with either of the two BASICs supplied with SOL I am still usually able to run the program in one of the other BASICs.

With thousands of scientific and statistical programs written in FORTRAN and a bank vault full of business/financial programs in COBOL, the appearance of FORTRAN and COBOL compilers for small computers has made them much more attractive to many users. The availability of PILOT interpreters for the PET, APPLE, TRS-80, and several other computers makes them more useful in educational settings since PILOT is a language specifically designed for computer assisted instruction.

Experienced programmers generally have their favorite language and feel most comfortable working in that language. The availability of such a wide variety of interpreters and compilers for microcomputers is one sign of emerging maturity in our field.

Applications Software

How does a writer summarize in a few short pages the tremendous variety of applications programs on the market today? It's a difficult, if not impossible, task. It is now 2:30 in the morning as I write this section of the book and I don't think I'll even try. A user can purchase software off the shelf for a variety of usual and unusual applications. The Instant Software people, for example, sell a program that helps design antennas for amateur radio operators, and another that helps design model rockets. Owners of small computers can take their choice of an almost endless variety of games, business applications, innovative home programs, and educational programs.

One of the best ways to get a current picture of the applications software that is available is to read the ads in current issues of the small computer magazines. When it is time to get serious about buying software, users should use several publications that have appeared recently and which make the job of finding good software for small computers a little easier. Several are listed and described below:

Periodical Guide for Computerists (E. Berg Publications, 14751 - 112th Ave. NE, Kirkland, WA 98033). Mr. Berg began the Guide in 1976. The original edition was for 1975-76. It consists of categorized listings of 1,812 articles published in the 15 magazines and journals most relevant to the small computer user. The $5 Guide provides readers with a means of finding articles on a variety of topics. Berg includes all the articles published in the magazines, not just those on software topics. Many of the 100 categories, however, are software related (business and accounting, games, text editing) and the Periodical Guide is a convenient way of locating an article on a particular topic. There is a Guide for 75-76, 1977, 1978, and 1979. They are available from E. Berg Publications and from Bits Inc., the book service of Byte Magazine.

Belais' Master Index to Computer Programs in BASIC (Falcon Publishing, 140 Riverside Avenue, Ben Lomond, California 95005). The Belais Index is a 192 page directory of BASIC programs which have been published in the computer magazines. It contains descriptions of 531 programs, all of which can be obtained simply by buying a copy of the magazine they appeared in. Each program is described in detail. For $7.95 it is well worth the price.

Schreier Software Index (Schrier Software Index, 4327 E. Grove Street, Phoenix, Arizona 85040). The first edition of this index covers programs published from January to June, 1978. Others issues are also available. Schrier's index covers both machine and higher level language programs which have appeared in magazines and books. The programs are indexed by category and by the type of computer they were written for. Each edition is $4.95 and well worth the price.

This chapter concludes the preliminary or introductory section of the book. In the following chapters you will be introduced to the art and science of programming computers. It is likely that many users will be content to buy prepackaged software written specifically for their system. There is certainly nothing dishonorable about that. Even a little knowledge about the way programs work, however, will make your computer a much more versatile and useful machine. Canned programs can be customized to suit your particular needs; programs written for other computers can be modified to work in yours, and unique needs can be met by writing your own software. The following chapters will help you take those first steps toward understanding small computer programming.

Chapter 4

Mr. Chips and the
Machine Language

Although we felt it made sense to put the machine and assembly language chapters at the beginning of the book, our logic was by no means compelling. Some computer hackers argue that learning about machine language programming first, before high level languages like BASIC, establishes a firm foundation upon which all other software training can be based. There is merit in that argument. Machine language requires the programmer to possess an intimate knowledge of the computer chip being used, its architecture, the chip's instruction set, and the way the entire computer system is interrelated. A person who understands the way machine language programs work in his or her system will probably have little difficulty programming in other languages using that same system. Only machine language puts the user in direct contact with the heart and soul of the computer — everything else puts something between the programmer/user and the ground zero goings-on inside the system.

But is machine language the place to start? Most newer small computers do not require machine language programming skills. A typical system will have an 8K or 12K BASIC in ROM which takes control of the computer as soon as power is turned on. Thousands of users aren't even aware, for example, of the machine language capabilities of computers such as the PET, APPLE, TRS-80, and Ohio Scientific models. It is entirely possible to get the computer to do many useful things without going beyond BASIC. BASIC is also easier to learn and easier to use than machine language.

If you are a beginner in the field of computer software and would like to get a fast start on learning a language that will allow you to quickly get the computer working on some game or business application, it makes sense to read chapters 6, 7, 8 and 9 now. They cover BASIC in some detail and provide guidelines on how to use the BASIC programs that are already published in books and computer magazines.

Those who have some knowledge of BASIC, those who own systems like the KIM that don't come with BASIC, and all you other masochists out there may find it more useful to read about machine language first before going on to high level programming.

CHIPS AND INSTRUCTION SETS

The heart of any microcomputer is the microprocessor chip, a small integrated circuit that contains the central processing unit, or CPU. The first microprocessor chip was the 4004, developed in 1971 by Intel. Intel also created the 8008, the first chip to attract significate attention in the small computer market. The 8080, descendent of the 8008, became the foundation for thousands of small computers that are still in use today. The 8080 chip requires three DC voltages to operate, +5, −5, and +12. It *understands* 78 machine instructions which are built into the chip itself. The ALTAIR, IMSAI, Processor Technology, and PolyMorphic computers were all part of the first wave of small computers that hit the market in the early seventies and all used the 8080 chip.

A significant competitor of the 8080 is the Z-80. It was developed by Zilog corporation, a venture begun by three engineers who left Intel to start their own company with financing provided by Exxon, the oil giant. The Z-80 is faster than the 8080, requires only a single +5 volt DC power supply, and understands 158 different machine instructions, 78 of which are the same ones the 8080 understands. Thus the Z-80 can run programs written for the 8080. Programs written for the Z-80, however, can be made more efficient than equivalent 8080 programs through the use of the Z-80's expanded instruction set. Computers using the Z-80 chip include the Radio Shack TRS-80 and the Exidy Sorcerer.

In addition to the 8080 and the Z-80 there are two other chips which have become very popular. The oldest is the 6800 chip from Motorola. The 6800 is somewhat similar to the 8080 but it requires only a +5 volt DC power supply. Southwest Technical Products is the best known manufacturer of small computers using the 6800 chip. The other popular chip is the 6502, from MOS Technology, a division of Commodore Business Machines. The 6502 bears a strong resemblance to the 6800; so strong, in fact, that the MOS and Motorola spent some time in court over the issue. The 6502 is used in several popular computers today including the PET, APPLE, and KIM.

There are many other microprocessor chips that have smaller followings, and each of the major chip manufacturers has come out with improved versions of their chips. Intel has the 8085, for example, which can be thought of as an improved 8080. Because of their dominant position in the market today, however, this chapter will concentrate on three chips — the 8080, the Z-80, and the 6502. Around 99% of the small computers in use today use one of the three, and enhanced versions such as the 8085 are very similar. It is not likely that the skills learned by working with any of these three will be totally obsolete anytime in the near future.

REGISTERS AND FLAGS

From the software viewpoint there are three things you should know about a computer chip. Each has an instruction set, each has a set of storage areas (registers), and each has a group of *status* bits or flags that change as conditions inside the chip change. Registers and flags will be discussed in this section while instruction sets will be presented in the next.

Figure 4-1 illustrates the register architecture of the 8080 microprocessor. Inside each microprocessor chip are special temporary storage locations which can be used to store data during program operations. Some of the registers have special functions while others are general purpose storage bins that can be used in a variety of ways by the programmer.

There are three special purpose registers on the 8080. The Accumulator or A register will hold one 8-bit byte of data, and is used to transfer data to and from the CPU chip. It can conveniently be thought of as a gate since it is the only way for data to get in or out of the chip. In addition, the accumulator is the only register which can be used to perform some arithmetic instructions.

The next special purpose register in the 8080 is the Program
Counter, or PC register. When a program is stored in memory
and executed, the computer will begin following the directions
of the program. The PC register keeps track of where the next
instruction is to come from. Suppose, for example, that a program has been stored in memory from CD00 to CE00 hex. To
run or execute the program the monitor command *EX CD00*
could be used on several computers. That command would
cause the number CD00 to be stored in the PC register. The instruction stored in memory location CD00 would then be executed and the PC register would be incremented as the program was run. After each instruction is carried out the computer
looks at PC to determine where to look in memory for the next
instruction. PC is a 16 bit register since it must hold 16 bit
binary memory addresses.

8080

REGISTER SET

Accumulator	Register A	7 S	6 Z	5 X	4 AC	3 X	2 P	1 X	0 C	Flag Register
8-Bit "Scratchpad registers"	Register B	Register C								
	Register D	Register E								More "Scratch-pad registers"
	Register H	Register L								
Special Pur-pose registers	Stack Pointer									
	Program Counter									

**Figure 4-1   A diagram illustrating
the internal registers of the 8080**

Another special 8080 register is the Stack Pointer or SP register. As a program is run it is often necessary to store numbers in
RAM memory for use later in the program. The SP register contains a 16 bit memory address that tells the CPU where the stack
is located. The 8080 instruction PUSH is used to place a number
on the stack while the instruction POP is used to retrieve a
number from the stack. More on PUSH and POP later.

There are also several general purpose or *scratchpad* registers in the 8080 (B, C, D, E, H, and L). Each of these registers can be used independently to store an 8 bit binary number. When it is necessary to deal with 16 bit numbers these registers can also be combined into three pairs (BC, DE, HL) using the appropriate instructions.

Another register in the 8080 is used to store *flag* data. The 8080 has five *flags* that indicate certain conditions within the computer. Suppose, for example, that an instruction is executed that involves subtracting 1011 from 1011. The result would be 0, and the Z flag or zero flag would be *set*. The Z flag is stored in the seventh bit of the flag register. It will be a *1* if the result of the last instruction was zero and a *0* if not.

The C or carry flag is stored in bit one of the flag register. It will be 1 if the last instruction required a carry to be performed from the highest order bit of a byte or if a borrow was required from that bit. An instruction to add 00001111 to 01011111 would not set the carry bit while 11001111 plus 01001111 would.

$$\left(\begin{array}{c} \text{Carry Flag} = 0 \\ 00001111 \\ +\,01011111 \\ \underline{0}\,01101110 \end{array}\right. \qquad \left(\begin{array}{c} \text{Carry Flag} = 1 \\ 11001111 \\ +\,01001111 \\ \underline{1}\,00011110 \end{array}\right.$$

There is also a parity flag or P which resides in the third bit position. The parity flag is set to 1 when all the ones and zeros in the flag register add up to an even number after an instruction is executed (see Chapter 2 for more on parity).

The other two flags are the S or sign flag and the AC or auxiliary carry flag. S is set to 1 if the result of the last instruction is a negative number. AC is set to 1 when a carry occurs out of bit 3 of the numbers being added. In the carry flag example above, note that in the auxiliary carry flag would be set in the example where the carry flag is not and vice versa. (Remember that *bit 3* is the fourth bit over from the right since the first bit is designated as *bit 0*.) You may well wonder why bit 3 is special enough to be singled out for individual attention. There is an 8080 instruction, DAA, which requires this information, to execute properly.

The Z-80 register architecture is shown in Figure 4-2. With the exception of two additional *index registers* the format for Z-80 registers is the same as for the 8080. Notice, however, that the Z-80 has *cloned* all the 8080 8 bit registers. There is an A and an A′, a B and a B′, and so on. Only the standard or the *cloned* set of Z-80 registers is operative at any given time. The register set used is selected by one of the Z-80's instructions.

Z-80

REGISTER SET

(Main)

		7	6	5	4	3	2	1	0	
Accumulator	Register A	S	Z	X	AC	X	P/O	N	C	Flag Register

	Register B	Register C
Register D	Register E
Register H	Register L

8-Bit "Scratchpad registers"

More "Scratchpad registers"

(Alternate)

		7	6	5	4	3	2	1	0	
Accumulator	Register A′	S	Z	X	AC	X	P/O	N	C	Flag Register

Register B′	Register C′
Register D′	Register E′
Register H′	Register L′

8-Bit "Scratchpad registers"

More "Scratchpad registers"

Index Register IX
Index Register IY
Stack Pointer
Program Counter

Figure 4-2 A diagram illustrating the internal registers of the Z-80

The Z-80 has two additional 16 bit registers that are not in the 8080. These are called *index* registers. Both the IX and IY register can be used to store a 16 bit number that designates a particular memory address. Suppose, for example, that a code conversion table is stored in memory starting at location D000. The Z-80 allows the programmer to store the 16 bit D000 in either IX or IY. Z-80 instructions that add an *offset* value to the value stored in IX or IY can now be used to obtain the correct memory address. An example will help clarify this process.

Suppose we come to a point in our code conversion program which calls for the value stored in memory location D00F to be loaded into the accumulator. The Z-80 instruction for that, written in hex, is 3A OF D0. (The reason for writing the address backwards will be explained later.) This is a *three byte* instruction; one byte is required to specify the instruction itself, and two more are needed to specify the memory address where the desired number is stored. If, however, D000 was stored in IX it would be possible to use a different instruction to accomplish the same thing: DD 7E 0F. The instruction DD 7E works the same as 3A 0F DO except it adds the number which follows (in this case 0F) to the value stored in IX to get the memory address required. This is called *indexed addressing*. In programs where this type of instruction must be used many times, the use of indexed addressing makes relocating the program to another area of memory, or another computer, far easier. It is only necessary to change the base number in IX to place the code table in a different memory location.

The Z-80 also has a set of flags, most of which duplicate the 8080 flags. There is a Carry (C), Zero (Z), and a Sign (S) flag, all of which work like their 8080 counterparts. The Z-80 also has a flag that is used for two purposes. The Z-80 Parity (P/V) flag is sometimes used to indicate whether the result of an instruction produced a number with odd or even parity. It is set to 0 if parity is odd, to 1 if parity is even. The P/V flag is also used under some circumstances to indicate whether a particular math operation produced an overflow—0 means no overflow; 1 means there was an overflow. Overflow is a term used in *two's complement* arithmetic to indicate the computation performed has modified, through a borrow or carry, the most significant bit (see chapter 2 for more details).

Another Z-80 flag is the add/subtract (N) flag. The N flag is set to 0 when an instruction adds decimal numbers. It is 1 when decimal numbers are subtracted. The final Z-80 flag is the H or half-carry flag. It works just like the 8080 AC flag.

Figure 4-3 illustrates the register architecture of the 6502 microprocessor. Like the Z-80 it has an X and Y index register as well as an accumulator, program counter, and stack pointer. There are no general purpose registers as are provided in the 8080 and Z-80. Instead, external memory locations are used for temporary storage of data. The 6502 also has seven flags, each of which is stored in a one bit location within the chip. The negative (N), overflow (V), zero (Z), and carry (C) flags are similar to the 8080 and Z-80 flags already discussed. The break (B) flag is set to 1 after a special instruction called BRK is executed. It causes the computer to interrupt its execution of instructions. The interrupt (I) flag can be set externally. It is used to interrupt program execution and then restart it. Finally, the decimal (D) flag is set when the microprocessor is required to perform a particular form of arithmetic called *binary coded decimal,* or BCD.

6502

REGISTER SET

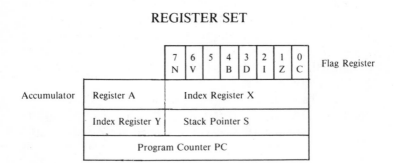

Figure 4-3   The 6502 register and flag pattern

INSTRUCTION SETS

The strategies involved in learning enough about machine language programming to use software written by others and to write short subroutines yourself are somewhat different from those called for if the goal is to become a completely independent machine language programmer. Most colleges and universities offer at least one, and often several, machine language courses which produce independent programmers. Such courses are hard work, and much of that work is not necessary if your goals for learning about machine language are more modest.

This chapter will cover much of what you should know if your goals are modest.

Figure 4-4 is part of a typical machine language program listing you might find in a magazine or book. Only a small section of the program is reproduced here, but it will serve nicely as an illustration:

0100	AF			0000	XRA	A
0100	D3	FE		0001	OUT	OFEH
0103	21	86	02	0002	LXI	H, 646D
0106	01	00	08	0003	LXI	B,2048D

Figure 4-4   Example of a machine language program

This section was taken from an 8080 program by Newtt Awl which appeared in *Access,* a now defunct magazine for users of Processor Technology equipment. The complete program, when executed, causes a small steam locomotive to come chugging across your screen with little o's of smoke billowing from its smokestack. Listings like this are common in the field; many describe very useful programs that may be of interest to you. Figure 4-4 contains everything found in a typical listing except the comments, which are often placed on the far right of each line. Comments usually include information that helps you decipher what the program is supposed to be doing.

The listing may look very complex and foreboding now if you haven't worked with machine language before, but it is not. Every instruction, regardless of what instruction set it came from, has four major pieces of information associated with it. Several pieces of that information are shown in Figure 4-4. Each instruction has been assigned a number. These numbers are decoded by the computer to make it execute the requested operations. Although the computer deals with binary numbers, most small systems allow the programmer to use hexadecimal numbers. We will also use hex numbers in this chapter and the one that follows. In Figure 4-4 the second column contains the numbers that designate the instructions to be executed. The numbers are hexadecimal. In the first line, for example, the part on the left looks like this:

0100 AF

The 0100 is the memory address where the instruction AF is to be placed. AF (175 in decimal) is the hexadecimal code which corresponds to the 8080 Exclusive OR instruction. AF tells the computer to perform an Exclusive OR using the number stored in the accumulator. Other 8080 instructions cause an Exclusive OR or XOR to be carried out on two numbers, one in the A register and one in another register. With AF, however, the XOR is between the number in the A register and itself. With XOR, which was described in Chapter 2, the only way to get a 1 as a result is for one of the values being used to be a 1 and the other a 0. Since the number in A is being XORed with itself that will not happen, and the A register will contain all zeros after the AF instruction is executed. In this program it is simply a way of ensuring that the A register contains zeros when the program is run. That first line also has some more information on it:

0110   AF   0001   XRA   A

The 0001 in the middle of the listing is just a line number. It helps you keep track of where you are in the program. To the right of 0001 is the cryptic phrase *XRA A*. That is a short mnemonic that means the same as AF. AF is called the Object Code and it is what the computer understands. XRA A is called the Source Code and is easier for the human user to understand. Each instruction has a number or Object Code value and a Source Code label.

If we wanted to enter the program in Figure 4-4 into the computer and run it, only the Object Code would be entered. On a Sorcerer computer, for example, it would be necessary to type *EN 100* and then press the RETURN key. The computer would then expect to receive sets of two digit hexadecimal numbers, each separated by a space. The first number which was typed in, AF in our example, would be placed in memory location 0100 hex, with succeeding two digit numbers being placed in memory at 101, 102, . . . etc. Since the computer's operating system software will automatically handle the assignment of data to memory locations it is not necessary to type in the memory column of the program. After *EN 100* only the pairs of hexadecimal numbers just to the right of the memory address line will be typed in. For the program in Figure 4-4 it would look like this:

EN 100 (CR)   CR means the carriage return is pressed.

AF D3 FE 21 86 02 01 00 08......and so on....../(CR)

After the entire program is entered, / is used to tell the Sorcerer you are finished entering the program. Then typing *EX 100* and pressing CR would cause the computer to go to memory location 100 and begin executing the instructions located there.

Notice in the second line of the program in Figure 4-4 that there are two hexadecimal numbers just after the memory location number (0101):

0101   D3 FE   0001   OUT   0FEH

D3 is an object code for an instruction whose source code label is OUT. OUT does just what it says, it sends an 8 bit binary number out of the chip to a particular destination. The number to be sent is located in the Accumulator. OUT by itself, however, does not specify the destination. OUT can be used to send data to many *ports,* something that will be discussed later in this chapter. OUT requires that the hexadecimal number which follows it specify which port the data is to be sent to. In the example, the data in the accumulator (8 zeros) will be sent to port FE. This is called a *two byte* instruction because it takes one byte for the instruction while a second is required to provide additional information needed to carry out the instruction.

Even an experienced programmer might not remember what D3 FE is supposed to accomplish, but it will not be long before OUT 0FEH will seem perfectly clear to you. The H at the end of OFE is just a reminder that it is a hexadecimal number. The FE which follows D3 is called an *operand.* Operands are listed just beyond the object code for the instruction on each line. Some instructions require no operands (e.g., AF in line 0000), while others require one, two, or three operands (e.g., 21 in line 0003 needs two operands).

The third line of the program has three hexadecimal numbers on it (21 86 02). The source code label for instruction 21 is LXI which, freely translated, means *load the 16 bit number which follows into the register pair HL.* If the 16 bit number is a memory address it is necessary to reverse the order of the two hexadecimal numbers which specify the address: 02 86 becomes 86 02. This is necessary because the first number will be placed in the L register and the second will go in the H register. If, however, the HL register pair is looked at later in the program to obtain a memory address, the data in the H register will be considered to have the 8 *highest order* bits with L containing the 8 *lowest order* bits. You may get used to this after a while, but you'll probably never like it. Notice that the decimal values of the operands have been placed in the far right column of lines 0003 and 0004.

Some while ago it was mentioned that each instruction has four major pieces of information associated with it. Two of them, the object code and source code labels, have already been noted. The third piece of information is the set of flags that can be affected by a particular instruction. Some instructions have no effect on any flag while others may potentially change several.

The fourth piece of information is the amount of time it takes for a particular instruction to be executed. We will not consider time at this point since beginning programmers are usually more concerned with the other three factors.

At this point in your reading you should refer to a book which describes the instruction set used by your computer. If you have an Apple, KIM, SYM, PET, or Atari computer the 6502 instruction set is your cup of tea. Horizon, Sorcerer, and TRS-80 owners need information on Z80 instructions while many older systems such as the Poly 88 and the Processor Technology Sol were built with 8080 chips. Southwest Technical Products computers use the 6800 chip. dilithium Press publishes several good books which introduce the reader to the intimate details of instruction sets. Several other publishers also offer similar texts. Look for a book that fits your own personal preferences, and one that provides the level of detail your interests require. Some books, for example, simply list the instructions, explain them, and give a few illustrative examples. Other books, on the same instruction set, go into great detail and provide hundreds of program examples which can be used by individuals who are writing their own software.

The examples which are used to illustrate points in the remainder of this chapter all use 8080 or Z80 instructions. If neither of these chips is of particular interest to you the examples will still be useful since they often illustrate general principles and procedures. Understanding how the examples work will make it easier for you to figure out instructions written in other machine languages.

HARDWARE DETAILS AND SOFTWARE OPERATION

Up to this point not much has been said about the hardware within which all the software operates. Up to a point it is possible to ignore the hardware and concentrate on getting the software to do what you want. Up to a point. Sooner or later the peculiar characteristics of your hardware intrudes on the way software operates and forces you to attend to it. The construction of a computer system from a collection of parts involves making choices between many options, each with advantages and disadvantages. The choices made, however, determine to some extent how and if a particular piece of software will work in the system.

There are four aspects of a computers hardware system which the user/programmer should be aware of: the memory map, I/O port and status assignments, the video display memory map, and significant memory locations and codes.

Memory Maps

Most of the computers sold today can accomodate a maximum of 64K of memory (there are schemes that allow more, but they are of little interest to home computer users. The typical system, however, will not come with all 64K installed. There may, in fact, be as little as 4K of RAM (or Random Access Memory). A typical system will also have at least one or two sections of ROM memory which is used to store the monitor program software and perhaps a BASIC interpreter. The location of RAM and ROM (or EPROM) in memory is the principal topic of a memory map.

TRS-80 Memory Map

A map of a TRS-80 computer with 16K of memory and Level II BASIC is shown in Figure 4-5. The first 12287 bytes of memory in the TRS-80 are used to store an excellent interpreter for

Radio Shack's Level II BASIC. Putting BASIC in ROM has
many advantages. It is always in memory, for example, since the
contents of ROM are not lost when the computer is switched
off. BASIC gives its friendly greeting every time the TRS-80 is
turned on.

Decimal Addresses		Hexadecimal Addresses
65535		FFFF
	Available For Memory Expansion	
32768		8000
32767	Stack Area	7FFF
	16K RAM	
16384		4000
16383	Video Display	3FFF
15360	Memory	3C00
15359	Dedicated	3BFF
12288	Addresses	3000
12287		2FFF
	Level II BASIC ROM	
00000		0000

Fig. 4-5 The TRS-80 Memory Map

A disadvantage of BASIC in ROM is the fact it takes up memory space even when it is not in use. The first 12K of memory will always be occupied by the BASIC interpreter, leaving a maximum of 48K for RAM. Individuals who, for example, use the TRS-80 for word processing may employ a machine language program such as the Electric Pencil. This is a popular piece of sophisticated word processing software that sells for $100 to $275, depending on the version. Since the Electric Pencil is a machine language program, it does not require BASIC to be in memory. Computers that store BASIC in RAM require BASIC to be loaded from tape or disk each time the computer is used, but they offer the advantage of being able to use the RAM area where BASIC normally resides for other purposes. A *16K* TRS-80 actually has over 37K in it, but only 16K is *user programmable.*

The memory map in Figure 4-5 shows just over 3000 bytes of memory between 12288 and 15360 which are *dedicated addresses.* Actually there is no memory in this section of the map. The TRS-80 uses some of these addresses for special purposes. For example, an instruction that *reads* memory location 37EB is really reading signals from a line printer if one is attached to the computer.

Printers send a variety of status signals back to the computer to indicate whether the printer is ready to receive data to be printed. LD A, 37E8H puts the status byte from the printer into the A register. If the printer being used puts a 1 in the 3rd bit when it is ready to print and a 0 when it is busy, additional instructions could be written to check the contents of the third bit before sending a character to the printer. Data going to the line printer is sent to 37E8. To the computer, it is just sending a character to a memory location. It does not know that 37E8 is no ordinary memory location. It is, instead, the address of the line printer.

How can the printer be connected to the computer as if it were a memory location? Essentially the circuitry of the computer and/or the printer interface is wired so that it is continually looking for the address 37E8 on the address lines. When 37E8 is found on the address lines, the signal on the 8 data lines is sent to the printer. This scheme is called memory mapped I/O. Some processor chips such as the 6502 use memory mapped I/O as the only means of connecting peripherals to the computer.

The TRS-80 has reserved the memory addresses from 3000H to 37FFH for memory mapped I/O addressing. Few of the addresses are actually used at present but there is plenty of room for later expansion. Bits which are sent to or retrieved from addresses in the area are, for example, used to activate the disk control circuitry, and to indicate which disk drive is to be used in systems that have one or more disk drives.

Just above 37FF hex on the TRS-80 memory map is another interesting area. The area from 3800 to 3880 hex is actually connected to the TRS-80 keyboard. Each key on the keyboard is treated as one bit of an 8 bit byte located at a memory address. The arrangement for two of the addresses is shown below:

Bit	0	1	2	3	4	5	6	7
Address								
3801	@	A	B	C	D	E	F	G
3802	H	I	J	K	L	M	N	O

The keyboard software in the TRS-80 ROM continually scans the memory addresses from 3801 to 3880 hex until a key is pressed. If no key is pressed, all these memory locations will be read as 0. A key press, however, will cause one bit in a particular memory address to change from 0 to 1. Pressing D, for example, will cause the computer to read a 1 in bit 2 of memory address 3801. Pressing N would produce a 1 in bit 6 of address 3802. Again, note that 3801 and 3802 are not connected to RAM or ROM, although the computer thinks they are. Instead, the keyboard is wired to the computer in such a way that it is treated as a series of memory locations by the TRS-80 software. This method of interfacing a keyboard uses very few parts but does take up some memory space.

There are two more sections of the TRS-80 memory map which should be mentioned now. Just above the keyboard area is a 1024 byte section of RAM that controls the video display. It starts at 3C00 hex and goes up to 3FFF. Each byte of memory in this area controls a section of the computer's video display. A diagram of the TRS-80 video display map is shown in Figure 4-6. The addresses are given in hex and decimal. If a particular

ASCII code is placed in memory location 3E40, for example, the character represented by that code will appear at the left hand margin of line 10 on the display.

	Hex	Decimal		
Line 1	3C00	15360		
2	3C40	15424		
3	3C80	15488		
4	3CC0	15552		
5	3D00	15616		
6	3D40	15680		
7	3D80	15744		
8	3DC0	15808		
9	3E00	15872		
10	3E40	15936		
11	3E80	16000		
12	3EC0	16064		
13	3F00	16128		
14	3F40	16192		
15	3F80	16256		
16	3FC0	16320		16383 3CFF

Fig. 4-6   Diagram of the TRS-80 Video Display

The TRS-80 display is typical of those used in many small systems. It can display a maximum of 16 lines with each line containing up to 64 characters. That means a total of 1024 characters can be on the screen at any one time. The software already in ROM will handle the job of displaying characters on the screen when BASIC is being used. Machine language programs for the TRS-80 must contain their own display routines, however. One way to do this is to load the ASCII code to be displayed into the accumulator. For example, the hex number, 2A, is the ASCII code for the star symbol (★). To display this symbol, you would use the following instruction:

LD A, 2AH

The instruction above loads the accumulator with 2A. The next step involves moving the contents of A to one of the video display memory addresses:

LD (3E80), A

When these two lines are executed, a " ★ " will appear on the left margin of the screen at the eleventh line.

As you can see from the previous discussion, addresses 0 to 3FFF (16383 decimal) in the TRS-80 memory map are occupied by ROM, dedicated RAM, or memory mapped I/O addresses. That means approximately 16K of the available 64K is not usable for programming or for storing language processors for other languages such as PILOT or FORTRAN. For most users, that is not a serious problem. Many programs will run quite nicely in far less than the 48K of RAM that can potentially be installed in the system above 3FFF. And with RAM for the TRS-80 selling for as little as $50 per 16K the cost of adding memory is not high. The price is a welcome contrast to the $700 I paid for my first 16K RAM board just a few years ago.

User RAM in the TRS-80 begins at 4000H and continues to 7FFH if only 16K of RAM is installed. The remainder of the memory map is unoccupied and available for expansion. As shown on the map, some of the RAM is used to store the *stack*. The stack is an area of memory where numbers that will be used later in the program are stored. The machine instruction PUSH is used to store data on the stack and POP is used to retrieve numbers from the stack.

Sorcerer Memory Map

Figure 4-7 illustrates the memory map of an Exidy Sorcerer computer with 32K of RAM installed.

The Sorcerer differs in several significant ways from the TRS-80. User RAM is at the bottom of the map rather than at the top. ROM and dedicated memory are grouped at the top. Whereas the TRS-80 has a permanently installed ROM that contains a BASIC interpreter and very limited software for loading and running machine language programs, the Sorcerer has an independent monitor program stored in 4K of ROM from E000 to EFFF. A small section of RAM at the top of the 32K is also used for the stack and for storing housekeeping data.

The Sorcerer stores its BASIC interpreter in 8K of ROM from C000 to DFFF. Physically this section of ROM is contained in a small cartridge that is inserted into the side of the computer. When the system is turned on the computer automatically jumps to the interpreter and prepares to work in BASIC. The BASIC-in-ROM for the Sorcerer differs from that on the

Decimal Addresses		Hexadecimal Addresses
65535	User Graphics RAM	FFFF
65024		FE00
65023	Standard Graphics	FDFF
64512		FC00
64511	ASCII PROM	FBFF
63488		F800
63487	Video Display RAM	F7FF
61568		F080
61567	Video Scratch RAM	F07F
61440		F000
61439	Monitor ROM	EFFF
57344		E000
57343	ROM PAC	DFFF
49152		C000
49151	Reserved for ROM and RAM	BFFF
32768		8000
32767	Monitor RAM	7FFF
32657		7F91
32656	Stack	7F90
32592		7F50
32591		7F4F
	32K RAM	
00000		0000

Fig. 4-7   The Sorcerer Memory Map

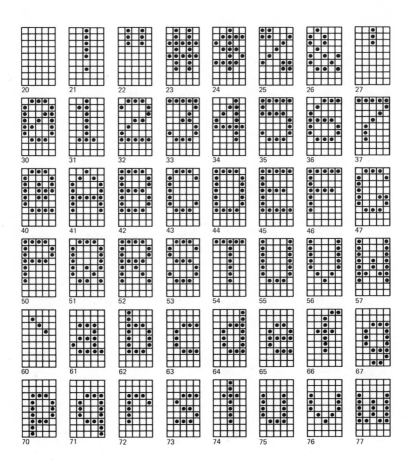

**Fig. 4-8(a) The MICRO-TERM ACT-V
9 by 5 display patterns**

TRS-80 because it is removable. Exidy sells ROM cartridges that contain other language processor (e.g., FORTRAN) and applications software such as an excellent word processing package. When another program is to be used, the BASIC cartridge is removed from the computer and the one containing the other program is inserted. This feature allows the 8K of memory addresses set aside for BASIC to be used for other software as well. In the Sorcerer, 24K of the memory map from 8000 to DFFF, is set aside for software-in-ROM cartridges.

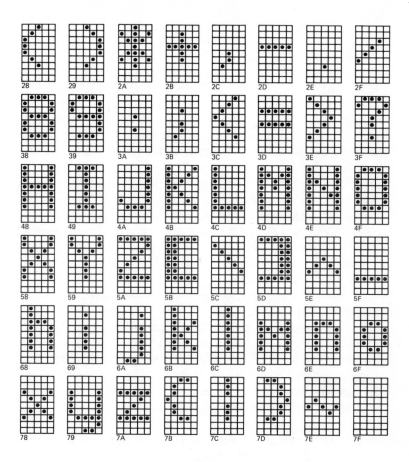

**Fig. 4-8(b)   The MICRO-TERM ACT-V
9 by 5 display patterns**

Several areas at the top of the memory map are used for housekeeping data and temporary data storage. There is a ROM from F800 to FBFF which contains the display character patterns for ASCII codes. The patterns for Sorcerer's extensive graphics character set are also stored nearby from FC00 to FDFF hex. Just above the graphics patterns is a section of memory that is reserved for *user defined graphics*.

Each character on the Sorcerer screen is made up of a pattern of dots. The dots are arranged in an 8 by 8 square with each square representing one character. There are thus 64 individual *dots* that can potentially be used to create a particular character on the screen. Each dot in the pattern can be turned on or displayed independently, thus allowing the user to create a variety of graphic characters. If all 64 dots were turned on, a small square would appear on the screen.

Terminals and microcomputers vary in the arrangement of dot patterns they use for a video display. The 8×8 pattern adopted by Exidy for the Sorcerer is one popular style. Figure 4-8 illustrates another approach—a 9 by 5 matrix which is used on the MicroTerm ACT-V terminal. Each letter and symbol which can be displayed has its own dot pattern. The number below each character is its ASCII code in hex.

The Sorcerer will display all the ASCII characters and a comprehensive set of graphics characters automatically when the appropriate keys on the keyboard are pressed. The Sorcerer uses a *dot matrix* system for video display much like that illustrated in Figure 4-8. The Sorcerer, as mentioned before, uses an 8×8 dot matrix instead of a 9×5.

The Sorcerer also allows the programmer to create new graphics patterns to suit a particular need. *Programmable graphics,* for example, can be used to design display characters for foreign languages such as Arabic or Russian. Each key on the Sorcerer keyboard, then, can be used to display a standard ASCII symbol, a standard graphics character, and a *user defined* graphics character.

The last section of the Sorcerer memory map to be discussed is the video display RAM. This computer displays 30 lines of 64 characters, almost twice as much as the TRS-80. This explains why the display RAM area of the Sorcerer (F080 to F7FF) takes up 1920 bytes instead of the 1024 used by the Radio Shack system. Figure 4-9 is a diagram of the Sorcerer video display with the display addresses of the left margin printed in the appropriate location. Sending an 8 bit code to memory location F560 will cause a character or graphic symbol to be displayed in the middle of the twentieth line.

KIM Memory Map

The KIM is a small, one-board computer that has become very popular in recent years because of its low price and the availability of inexpensive software for it. Figure 4-10 illustrates

64 Characters

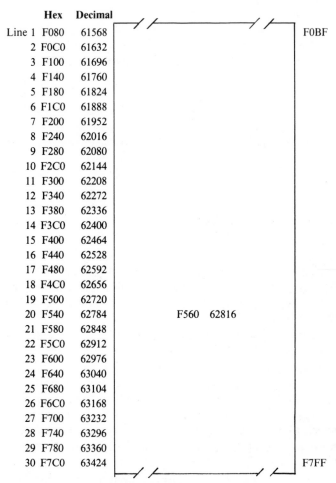

	Hex	Decimal
Line 1	F080	61568
2	F0C0	61632
3	F100	61696
4	F140	61760
5	F180	61824
6	F1C0	61888
7	F200	61952
8	F240	62016
9	F280	62080
10	F2C0	62144
11	F300	62208
12	F340	62272
13	F380	62336
14	F3C0	62400
15	F400	62464
16	F440	62528
17	F480	62592
18	F4C0	62656
19	F500	62720
20	F540	62784
21	F580	62848
22	F5C0	62912
23	F600	62976
24	F640	63040
25	F680	63104
26	F6C0	63168
27	F700	63232
28	F740	63296
29	F780	63360
30	F7C0	63424

F0BF

F560   62816

F7FF

**Fig. 4-9   Diagram of the Exidy
Sorcerer Video Display**

the memory map of the *bare* KIM, that is a KIM with no
memory other than that already on the KIM printed circuit
board. As you can see, there is very little memory in a bare
KIM. It has 1K or 1024 bytes of RAM memory from 0000H to
03FFH. And even in that 1K there are some memory addresses
which are reserved for use by the KIM operating system soft-

ware. The stack starts at 01FFH and develops downward in RAM to 0100 as numbers are added to it. There is also a small section of RAM (108 bytes) at 1780H to 17EBH which can be used for programming. Just above 17EB is another RAM area that is used by the KIM operating system (OS) software. The OS itself is stored in 2K of ROM from 1800H to 1FFF, while the area from 2000 to FFF is unused, but available for later expansion.

Two other areas on the memory map complete the bare KIM picture. A section from 1740 to 177F is used by the OS for memory mapped I/O addressing. There is no memory in this area. Instead the board is wired so that I/O devices such as the hex keyboard and the LED display that are on the board are connected to the CPU through these addresses (1740H through 1743H). In this section also, are the addresses of two timers. A timer is a circuit that generates a regularly changing output with a known time for each cycle. These cycles can be used to time the operation of the computer. For example, the system might be instructed to wait for 2 million cycles of one of the timers before processing the instructions that follow. (These timers go through a cycle very quickly; a wait of 2 million cycles is not really that long.)

Just below the system I/O area is a small section of addresses that have been reserved for use by the programmer who wants to communicate with an input and/or output device. There is one *port* on the KIM which is called *PAD* located at 1700H. Another port, called PBD, is at 1702H. Both PAD and PBD can be used to output data from the CPU or to input data to the CPU. Note that the KIM uses memory addresses for ports while the 8080 and Z-80 have a separate port system with a different set of numbers.

The ports on the KIM can be either output or input ports, but not both at the same time. There are two other memory addresses which control the two ports. Address 1701H is used to control PAD. If a *1* is placed in all eight bits of 1701, PAD will be treated as an output port. If, however, the byte 00001100 were sent to 1701H, PAD could be used as an input port on bits 0, 1, 5, 6, and 7 while bits 2 and 3 would be output. The other port, PBD at 1702H, is controlled by 1703H in a similar fashion.

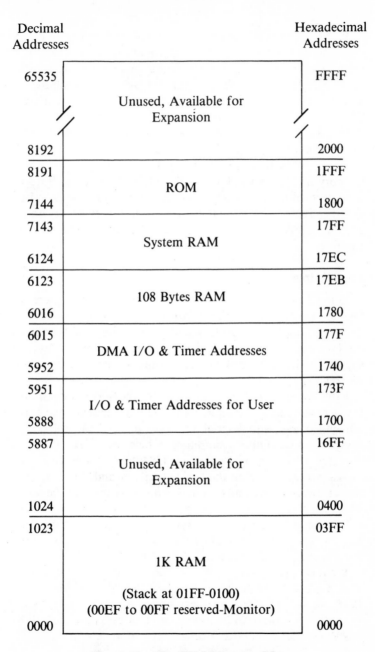

Decimal Addresses		Hexadecimal Addresses
65535	Unused, Available for Expansion	FFFF
8192		2000
8191	ROM	1FFF
7144		1800
7143	System RAM	17FF
6124		17EC
6123	108 Bytes RAM	17EB
6016		1780
6015	DMA I/O & Timer Addresses	177F
5952		1740
5951	I/O & Timer Addresses for User	173F
5888		1700
5887	Unused, Available for Expansion	16FF
1024		0400
1023	1K RAM (Stack at 01FF-0100) (00EF to 00FF reserved-Monitor)	03FF
0000		0000

Fig. 4-10   The KIM Memory Map

That completes the description of the KIM memory map. The three maps described in this section illustrate the variety in memory allocations and show why it is very difficult to transfer long machine language programs from one computer to another, even when the same chip is used in both computers. The Exidy Sorcerer and the TRS-80, for example, both use the Z-80 chip. The user RAM in a Sorcerer, however, is placed at the bottom of the memory map while the TRS-80 has its ROM with BASIC in that area. Other differences involve the use of memory addresses for I/O on the TRS-80 while the Sorcerer uses port addresses. With machine langue programs written specifically for the computer you own, however, an understanding of its memory map will make it easier to get a program running.

Port Addresses

In most of the manuals that come with computers there will be one or more lists of *port addresses.* There may also be a list or two of important memory addresses; these usually indicate the location of subroutines that perform a particular function such as sending a byte of data to a printer or inputing data from the keyboard.

Table 4-1 is a list of port addresses for the Sorcerer computer. It will be used as an example in this section since even the barest Sorcerer comes with a serial and a parallel port as well as two cassette ports. Other computers which cost less than the Sorcerer often achieve their price advantage by omitting some of the port circuitry on the basic computer and, instead, offer the hardware needed as optional equipment that can be added later. If your computer is not a Sorcerer the next few sections will not apply directly to your system. An understanding of the way the Sorcerer is set up, however, will make it easier to figure out the complexities of other computers.

What is a port? In computerese the term *port* is used much as it is in standard English. A port is a place where ships dock to load and unload cargo. In the computer a port is a place where the CPU can load or unload (input and output) data. One of the most obvious devices to connect to a port is a printer. The Sorcerer has provisions for connecting either a serial or a parallel printer through the appropriate port. At the back of the

Table 4-1   Sorcerer Port Allocations

Number	Function
FF	Parallel Data Port

FE	Parallel Status Port
	   Bit 6 data acknowledged (input)
	   Bit 7 data available (output)

FC	Cassette and Serial Data Port

FD	Cassette and Serial Status Port
	   Bit 0 buffer empty
	   Bit 1 data available

FE	Cassette and Serial Status Port
	   Bit 4 motor control #1
	   Bit 5 motor control #2
	   Bit 6 Baud rate (0 = 300; 1 = 1200)
	   Bit 7 0- sends data to cassette
	          1- sends data to serial connector

Sorcerer are two 25-pin connectors which are used to conveniently attach printers (or other devices). Generally those connectors will be called *ports* although, more correctly, the port is more than just the connector at the rear of the computer. A detailed look at the parallel port on the Sorcerer may make things a little clearer.

The Sorcerer uses the Z-80 IN and OUT instructions to send data to and from the CPU. An OUT instruction requires that the address of the port to which data is to be sent be specified right after the OUT instruction. The Z-80 in the Sorcerer uses 8 bits for I/O *port* addressing. This means any binary number from 00000000 (0 decimal) to 11111111 (255 decimal) can be used as a port address. The Sorcerer has been wired in such a way that the parallel port is assigned the address FF hex (11111111 in binary). When an OUT instruction is followed by FF the computer sends an 8 bit byte to the parallel port. Each of the 8 bits transmitted will be present on one of the 25 pins of the parallel connector on the back of the Sorcerer. The manual for this computer tells us where each bit is sent when an OUT FF instruction is executed:

Bit	Pin
0	16
1	17
2	18
3	19
4	7
5	6
6	5
7	4

The operator's manual for any parallel printer will provide instructions on how to hook up the printer to a computer. Since pin to bit assignments vary, however, you must know the assignments shown above in order to correctly connect the cable from the printer to the parallel port. In addition, if you want to write or adapt any software that outputs parallel data it will be necessary to know the address assigned to the parallel port (e.g., FF on the Sorcerer).

Since some printers also have keyboards on them, parallel ports often include the circuitry for input as well as output. When the Sorcerer is told to look for input from the parallel port (port FF) it looks for an 8 bit byte on the following pins:

Bit	Pin
0	10
1	22
2	11
3	23
4	12
5	24
6	13
7	25

Notice in Table 4-1 that there is a *Parallel Data Port* and a *Parallel Status Port*. Thus far the discussion has focused on the data port, FF. Parallel devices use a process called *handshaking* to control the flow of data through the data port.

Handshaking, in its simplest form, uses two signals to indicate when data can be transmitted. Parallel printers send a *data acknowledged* signal back to the computer when they have received a byte of data. One of the wires connecting the printer to the computer will have a *1* on it indicating it is ready to receive a character. When a character arrives, the printer will lower the line to a *0* to indicate it is busy printing. Once the character is printed and the printer can take another one, that line will change back to *1,* telling the computer it is o.k. to send another character.

No printer can type characters as fast as the computer can send them, thus the need for handshaking. The computer will not send more data to the parallel port until the printer signals that it is ready. Some systems may actually call this a READY signal. The Sorcerer will wait until it sees a *1* on the data acknowledged or Ready line before transmitting more data. Other computers expect to see the reverse, a *1* when the printer is not ready and a *0* when it is. It is not difficult to route the signal through a 20 cent integrated circuit that *inverts* it if your printer uses one convention and your computer the reverse.

On the Sorcerer the Data Acknowledged line from the printer must be connected to pin 2 of the parallel I/O connector. That pin is assigned to port FE, bit 6. The software in the Sorcerer will tell the CPU to took at port FE, bit 6, before it sends data to the parallel port. If bit 6 on port FE is a 0 the software goes into a loop and continues looking at the bit until it changes to a *1.* At that point a character is sent to the parallel port and thus is transmitted to the printer.

The parallel status port, FE, also has another signal on it called *Data Available.* It is on pin 9 of the connector. When the computer is told to look for data on the input pins of the parallel connector it first looks at port FE, bit 7. If that bit is 0, the CPU assumes that no new data is on the input pins of the parallel port. It will only accept data on those pins if bit 7 of port FE (pin 9) is a *1.* Thus, if you plan to input data to the computer via the parallel connector it is necessary to connect a *strobe* line to pin 9 as well as connecting 8 data lines. The strobe line should normally carry a *0* unless a key is pressed. At that point the keyboard should send the appropriate data to the computer on the 8 data lines; it should also send a strobe signal (*1*). When the Sorcerer receives the strobe signal it inputs whatever signals are on the data lines to the CPU.

Seems quite complicated doesn't it? It has given me a headache just writing all this out for you. If I tilt my head to one side I think bit 5 will fall out of my ear! And even with all this detail I have described only the simplest parallel port arrangement. Some systems add two or more additional status signals to keep everything marching along in the proper pattern. Enough of this though: let's look at the serial port.

The Sorcerer has assigned the hex number FC to the serial port. Near the parallel port's 25 pin connecter on the back of the computer is another connector which is used for serial devices. Slow printers and modems are the most commonly used serial devices. A serial port has only one data line going out and one going in, whereas the parallel port has 8 input and 8 output lines. Serial data transmission involves sending data out one bit at a time instead of sending the 8 bits of a byte out simultaneously. If you are unfamiliar with serial and parallel data transmission you may want to read relevant sections of the *Peanut Butter and Jelly Guide to Computers* or another introductory hardware text.

The Sorcerer uses pin 2 of the serial connector to transmit data out of the computer and pin 3 to input data. This computer, like most, uses the *RS232* format for serial data transmission. Again, an introductory hardware book will explain what this means if you are unfamiliar with the term. Essentially, RS232 is an electronics industry standard that many companies use when building equipment. In the most commonly used RS232 format a *1* is − 3 to − 9 volts while a *0* is + 3 to + 9 volts. A device that is *RS232* compatible can be connected to other equipment that uses the same standard with little difficulty. Most modems, the devices used to connect small computers and terminals to large mainframe computers, are RS232 compatible.

If we were connecting the Sorcerer to a modem we would need at least three lines: a ground, a transmit data line, and a receive data line. There is a ground on pin 1 of the serial connector; pin 2 handles outgoing data, and pin 3 accepts incoming data. The VEN-TEL AC103 modem, which can be used with the Sorcerer, has a ground on pin 7 of its connector, while it receives data on pin 3 and transmits data on pin 2. In order to connect the Sorcerer to the modem a cable with the following connections would have to be constructed:

Sorcerer Pin	Modem Pin
1 Ground	7 Ground
2 Data Out	3 Data In
3 Data In	2 Data Out

The Sorcerer uses port FD as a serial status port. Data sent to this port is used for a variety of purposes. Most of the work, however, is done automatically by circuits inside the Sorcerer. When the serial port (it also serves as the cassette port) is used to input data, bit 0 of port FD indicates when the buffer which contains the data to be input is empty — that is, there is no new data to be brought from the port to the CPU. Bit 1 of port FD goes high (1) when the buffer is available to transmit data. Bits 2, 3, and 4 go high when any of three types of errors occur in the data transmission. Since error checking is handled automatically, programmers will not usually be required to deal with this aspect of the Sorcerer directly.

The same status bits are used for different purposes when serial data is output from the computer. They can be used to determine how many bits are to be output in the data byte. Some printers, for example, expect to receive only 7 bits instead of the normal 8. Others may use only 6. The status bits can also be set to transmit data with even, odd, or no parity, and bit 2 of port FD can be set to specify the number of *stop bits* transmitted. When serial data is transmitted there will usually be 8 bits of data. Each of those bits will be a 1 or a 0. In addition there will be a *start* bit which is placed in front of the actual data by the computer. The start bit will be a 1. Following the 8 data bits will be one or two *stop* bits. The stop bits are zeroes, and devices differ in the number they expect to find in serial data.

As noted earlier the serial port is also the cassette output port on the Sorcerer. If bit 7 of port FE is set to 1, data will be sent to the serial connecter. If bit 7 is a 0, data will go to the cassette recorder connector.

The Sorcerer can transmit and receive data at two speeds — 300 Baud and 1200 Baud. A speed of 300 Baud means the computer will transmit 300 bits per second. If there are 8 bits of data per character plus one stop bit and one start bit — 10 bits total, that means 300 Baud is the same as 30 characters per second. At five characters to an average word that works out to about six words a second, 360 words a minute. A data transmission speed of 300 Baud is reasonably fast when compared to the average secretary. The LA-36 Decwriter II from Digital Equipment Corporation prints at 300 Baud and is considered very acceptable for light to moderate printing loads.

Some cassette storage systems also operate at 300 Baud. A reasonably long program, stored at 300 Baud on a cassette, may take as long as five or ten minutes to load. That is very slow for a cassette system, and few systems today run at that speed. The Sorecerer offers users the option of selecting the 300 Baud speed for either the serial port or the cassette port. Both are set to the 300 Baud speed by putting a zero in bit 6 of port FE. The 300 Baud speed is dependable, though slow. It is also the only speed many modems and printers can use. For all except the most crucial cassette storage uses, however, the Sorcerer's faster speed, 1200 Baud, will be preferred. This Baud rate works out to 120 characters per second, or 1440 words per minute. That's more like it. The faster Baud rate is selected by setting bit 6 to *1*. The Sorcerer's operating system software automatically selects the faster Baud rate for you when the computer is switched on.

IMPORTANT MEMORY ADDRESSES

The operating system software of a computer already contains instructions to do many of the routine jobs that must be done in any new software written for the computer. Many programmers take advantage of the existing routines when writing new programs. The Sorcerer operating system software, for example, has routines to input data from the keyboard and transmit data to serial and parallel printers. There is no need, then, to write these routines all over again in new software. In fact, some of the machine language software that is available today does not contain its own input/output routines. Instead, the software expects buyers to be able to patch in *jumps* to the I/O routines in the computer's operating system. This patching operation requires a knowledge of just where your computer's I/O subroutines are located and how they work.

A final reason for identifying the locations of subroutines in your OS software is the additional flexibility it gives the user. Suppose, for example, that your BASIC interpreter is located in memory from 0000 to 2000. Most BASICs will begin operating when they are executed at their lowest memory address. For many systems that would be 0. Executing BASIC at 0, however, means the interpreter will probably perform a *cold start*. A cold start requries the program to clear out all the RAM used for programming, reset the flags and registers to standard values and then tell the user it is ready to work. If you have a long program in the RAM area that the BASIC interpreter clears on a cold start, that program will be permanently lost. Most BASICs also have at least one *warm start* location. Entering at the warm start address gets you back into BASIC but does not destroy any program that was stored in RAM. Knowing the warm start address for your computer can save you a great deal of frustration and extra work. Let's look now at a specific computer, the Sorcerer.

Entry or Jump Addresses

Initial Entry Points for BASIC

E000 hex

This is the cold start entry point. Typing EX E000 and a carriage return when the Sorcerer is under the control of its operating system software lets the BASIC interpreter take control. First it searches through RAM, finds the highest contiguous RAM address that is available for use, sets aside a few bytes at the top of RAM for the stack, and then clears all the RAM from the stack area down. That means any program stored in RAM area will be lost. BASIC also clears the video display, sets the Baud rate at 1200, and prints READY on the screen.

E003 hex

This is Sorcerer's warm start address. BASIC can be entered at this address without disturbing any parameters already set (e.g., if the Baud rate has been set to 300 previously it will not be reset to the default value of 1200). Most important, perhaps, is the fact that RAM will not be cleared if BASIC is entered at E003 and any program already in RAM will not be lost. Data displayed on the screen will also remain undisturbed.

Input/Output Subroutine Addresses

The Z-80 instruction set has a pair of instructions, CALL and RETurn, which are used to access subroutines. A subroutine is a section of instruction code that performs a specific job. If the job done by the subroutine is one which must be accomplished many times during the execution of the program it is more efficient to write the subroutine once, rather than writing the code for the subroutine every time it is used in the program. A CALL instruction can be inserted instead.

Suppose, for example, that you have a machine language program that requires the keyboard of the computer to be checked, and the ASCII code for any key that has been pressed to be placed in the accumulator. With the Sorcerer, the instruction CALL E018 will accomplish this since EO18 hex is the address of the keyboard input subroutine in the Sorcerer operating system. When a CALL is executed the computer branches to the address specified after CALL. Before doing that, however, it places the memory address of the instruction just after CALL on the stack. The keyboard input routine located at E018 contains all the code necessary to scan the keyboard input circuits and find which key has been pressed. After placing the proper byte in the accumulator, this subroutine ends with a RET instruction. RET causes the computer to look at the memory address stored on the stack and jump back to it. Program execution then continues from there.

Using CALL and RET allows the use of already existing subroutines without even the necessity of typing them into your new machine language software. It is only necessary to know the address of the subroutine and to have some idea of how it works. CALL and RET can, of course, also be used with subroutines you write yourself. They are a very convenient pair of instructions.

The list below contains some of the more important subroutines in the Sorcerer. All have a RET at the end of the subroutine:

E009 hex

This address is the start of a general purpose input subroutine. The Sorcerer allows the current input device to be specified by the user with the monitor SET command. SET I = K, for example, instructs the computer to use the keyboard as the input device. P signifies the parallel port, and S the serial/recorder port. The SET command can also be used to provide an address (e.g., SET I = 1000) where a personalized input routine is stored. The input subroutine which begins at E009 will use whatever port or address has been specified by the SET command. If the parallel port has been designated as the current input device, the input subroutine will look to the parallel port for a byte of data. If it finds some valid data there, it will put the byte in the accumulator and then return to the program that CALLed the subroutine. This subroutine affects three registers and flags in the microprocessor. One is, of course, the A register or accumulator. That is where the input byte will be stored. The Z flag is also set to *1* even if there is no valid data to be input. Finally, the way the subroutine works will also affect other flag bits. If your program is using the flag bits, it will be necessary to store them somewhere else (perhaps on the stack using a PUSH instruction) before the CALL instruction is executed. After the subroutine has been executed and the RETurn instruction sends the computer back to the main program, the flags can be restored to their original condition (perhaps with a POP instruction).

E00C hex

This is the beginning of Sorcerer's general purpose output subroutine. It works much like the input subroutine described above. The byte of data in the A or accumulator register when a CALL E00C is executed will be sent to the current output device. No registers are changed when this subroutine is called, and there is an automatic delay (controlled by the SET S = ## monitor command) or pause before the RET instruction is executed. The delay is built in to prevent the computer from transferring data quicker than the destination device can accept it.

E018 hex

As mentioned previously this is the beginning of the keyboard input subroutine. Calling E018 places the ASCII code for the key pressed in the A register. If a keypress is detected the Z flag is set to *1;* if no key is pressed the Z flag is reset to *0.*

E01B hex

The last subroutine location to be discussed is the one used to access the video display. When E01B is called the byte of data in the A register is printed on the video display at the point on the screen where the cursor is displayed. No registers or flags are affected. Each of the valid ASCII codes for letters, numbers, and symbols will produce the appropriate symbol on the screen (e.g., a 62 hex in the A register will cause a lower case *b* to appear on the screen). In addition, the Sorcerer also prints a wide range of graphics characters when the proper code is sent to the video display circuit. There are also nine *video control* codes that are interpreted by the Sorcerer as instructions to modify the video display. The codes, in hex, are:

0A

When this code, the line feed, is sent to the video display the cursor will move down one line on the display. If it is already at the bottom of the display the top line will *scroll* off the screen.

0C

This code, the form feed, clears the screen display and places the cursor in the upper left corner of the display.

0D

The return code, moves the cursor to the left margin of the current line.

01

Moves the cursor over one space to the left but does not erase characters as it moves.

08

Moves the cursor over one space to the left and erases the character in the new position.

11

Places the cursor in the upper left corner (the home position) of the display.

13

Moves the cursor one space to the right.

17

Moves the cursor up one line.

A SAMPLE MACHINE LANGUAGE PROGRAM

The final section of this rather long discourse on machine language programming will be devoted to a short subroutine that enables the Sorcerer to output data to a serial printer. This subroutine, written in Z-80 machine language, is used in our microcomputer lab at Texas Tech University to interface the Sorcerer with a DecWriter II that runs at 300 Baud. Because the subroutine is a typical one, it will be considered in some detail. All the instructions will be explained in this section. Consult a Z-80 instruction set manual for a further explanation of the instructions.

The subroutine is placed in memory starting at 1000H or 4096 decimal. That is a convenient location for some of our work. At other times it is necessary to load the program into a different area of memory. The subroutine is listed in Table 4-2. It assumes the DecWriter II has been properly connected to the 25 pin serial connector on the Sorcerer. In Table 4-2 the memory addresses, in hex, are on the left; the machine language instructions, also in hex, are next, and the assembly language or source code equivalents are presented on the right.

There are several ways this subroutine can be accessed. The easiest way is to use the SET command in the Sorcerer operating system software. *Set O = 1000* instructs the Sorcerer to jump to a subroutine which begins at 1000H each time it has a character to be output. The jump will be in the form of a Z-80 CALL instruction. When Sorcerer arrives at the subroutine it will have the ASCII code for the character to be output in the A register. Why? Because the software in the Sorcerer is set up that way. Now let's look at each instruction in the printer subroutine.

F5   PUSH AF

F5   PUSH AF

Table 4-2   Serial Printer Driver Routine

1000	F5	PUSH	AF
1001	F5	PUSH	AF
1002	3E 60	LD	A,60H
1004	D3 FE	OUT	OFEH,A
1006	F1	POP	AF
1007	CD 12 E0	CALL	E012
100A	DB FD	IN	A, 0FDH
100C	CB 47	BIT	0,A
100E	CA 0A 10	JP	Z, 100AH
1011	AF	XOR	A
1012	D3 FE	OUT	OFEH,A
1014	F1	POP	AF
1015	C9	RET	

The contents of the registers A and F are put on the stack (an area of RAM reserved for temporary storage). The SP, or Stack Pointer, register pair will contain the 16 bit address of the memory location where the last of the two bytes (one from A, one from F) are stored after AF is executed. If SP contains 7F80 before the F5 instruction, it will contain 7F7E afterward. The contents of the A register will be in 7F7F and the contents of F (F is really the flag bits) will be in 7F7E. Remember that the stack is built from the top down. Each new entry is added to the stack at the next lower memory location in the stack RAM area. A is the accumulator register. PUSH AF is a way of stashing the contents of the accumulator and the flag bits in a convenient place from which they can be retrieved later. AF is put on the stack twice for reasons you will understand in just a moment.

3E 60   LD A,60H

This instruction loads register A with the number 60H.

D3 FE   OUT 0FEH,A

The contents of register A are sent to port FE. FE is the status port for the serial I/O and the cassette I/O. The number 60H in register A is 11000000 in binary. The seventh bit of FE determines whether data is sent to the serial port or the tape I/O circuit. This instruction sets bit 7 to *1* which means data will go to the serial port and thus to our printer. Setting bit six to *1* tells the computer to transmit data at 300 Baud.

F1	POP AF

The contents of the A and F register were stored on the stack a few instructions ago. F1 puts the data back in A and F. Now the ASCII code for the character to be printed is in the A register.

CD 12 E0	CALL E012

This CALL instruction sends the computer to memory address E012, the location of a subroutine which will output data in serial form to either the tape recorder or the serial port. The bits on the serial status port have already been set so that the byte in the accumulator will be sent out the serial port at 300 Baud.

DB FD	IN A, FD

A byte is input from FD into the A register. FD on the Sorcerer is a status port for the serial I/O port.

CB 47	BIT 0,A

This instruction is one of several in the Z-80 set that can be used to test a single bit. This particular one tests bit 0 in register A. If that bit is a 0, the Z flag is set to *1*; if the bit is 1, the Z flag is reset to *0*. Bit 0 from port FD is the status bit that indicates whether there is anything in the *transmit data buffer*. In essence, this status bit will be *1* while the computer is in the process of sending data out the serial port. It goes to *0* when the character has been transmitted. Note, however, that when the bit is 1 the Z flag is 0 (indicating the bit is not 0) and when the bit is 0 the Z flag is 1 (indicating the bit is indeed 0). Who the hell ever thought up this stuff anyway?

CA 0A 10	JR Z,100AH

This is a conditional jump instruction. If the Z or zero flag is reset (0) the jump instruction is ignored. In this program the zero flag will be 1 as soon as the printer can take another character to be printed. Thus, the only time the jump instruction will be obeyed is when the transfer process has not been completed. Where will the program jump to? That is determined by the number which follows CALL. In this case it is 100A, the start of the input instruction IN A, 0FDH which looks at the serial status port. The computer will loop through the instructions between 100A and 1010 until the Z flag is 0.

AF   XOR A

The AF instruction performs an Exclusive OR between the number in register A and itself. The end result is all zeroes in A.

D3 FE   OUT FE,A

The zeros in the accumulator are sent out to the status port. A 0 in bit 6 will cause output to go to the tape recorder connector, a 0 in bit 7 sets the speed of transfer at 1200 Baud. If no more characters are to be printed this instruction returns the computer to its standard serial port condition (e.g., recorder I/O at 1200 Baud).

F1   POP AF

Again registers A and F are loaded with data from the stack. This is the second POP AF, which is why the subroutine began with two PUSH AF instructions. At this point registers A and the flag bits will be exactly as they were when the subroutine was called.

C9   RET

The RETurn instruction sends the computer back to the program that called it. If there is another character to be printed, the whole process will begin again as another CALL 1000H will be executed with the next character to be printed in register A. If, however, there are no more characters to be printed the calling program moves on to the next instruction in its own sequence.

This concludes the chapter on machine language programming. You've come a long way toward being able to read, understand, and use machine language programs. The next chapter is concerned with a close relative of machine language — assembly language. Because of their intimate relationship (Aha! Scandal even in a computer book!) much of the material in the next chapter will reinforce learning begun in this one.

CHAPTER 5

A Better Way — Assembly Language Programming

Programming in the language of the computer chip is like drinking a fine wine, you have to acquire a taste for it. (Some of us, however, will always prefer Coors to Chateau Rothschild.) Machine language does put the programmer in direct contact with the computer, but it is also tedious, and something that must be practiced regularly if the skill is to be maintained at a high level. On the other hand, programming in a high level language is relatively fast, much easier to understand, and less likely to be forgotten if used intermittently.

Most readers will find a language like BASIC more suited to their needs than machine language, but there are some situations that call for its use even if most of the software for a project is written in BASIC. One example involves the use of graphics in programs for computers like the TRS-80 and the Atari 800. Many games, and some educational software, use the graphics features of small computers to draw game boards (e.g., checkers, chess, backgammon), graphs, and charts via BASIC commands. SET (64,21), for example, will cause a small white rectangle to be placed in the middle of the TRS-80 screen. The short program below will cause a line to be drawn across the TRS-80 screen about two inches from the bottom.

```
10 FOR X = 1 TO 127
20 SET (X,35)
30 NEXT X
```

The problem with most graphics drawn using BASIC instructions is that they tend to be drawn rather slowly. BASIC sacrifices speed for convenience, a tradeoff that is usually acceptable. The computer, even when running in BASIC, is still fast. If there is a great deal of detail in the graphics to be used, however, it may be necessary to write the graphics routines in machine language in order to speed things up a bit.

Another situation that often calls for a machine language program is interfacing the computer to a printer, especially if the printer is a surplus unit that does not use the ASCII code.

Computer users who only rarely need to write machine language programs will probably find it most convenient to write them out by hand, then enter and debug them using the commands in the computer's monitor or operating system software. For those who find themselves regular dabblers in the occult arts of machine language programming, however, it may be wise to consider moving up to assembly language. Even those who do not intend to do any work in machine or assembly language can profit from learning how it is done. Many of the program listings in the computer magazines are the products of an assembler — a program used to develop original software. Understanding those listings is a must if you want to use the programs they describe in your own system.

An assembly language is a low level language, very similar to machine language, with one major difference. The elements of an assembly language (the SOURCE CODE) are selected because they are easy for programmers to understand, while machine language (the OBJECT CODE) is what computers understand. The 8080 machine language instruction, 57 hex, has its counterpart in 8080 assembly language. It is MOV D,A which means "Move the contents of the A register into the D register." A programmer who sees MOV D,A in a listing will be much more likely to understand what it means than the same programmer who sees only the number 57.

Assembly language can be used by itself to write programs that are later translated into machine language by hand. It is more common and more convenient, however, to write assembly language programs using a piece of software called an assembler. Assemblers take programs written in assembly language ("SOURCE CODE") and translate them into machine language ("OBJECT CODE").

The major advantage of writing programs in assembly language is their degree of transparency; that is, you can more clearly see what a program is supposed to do. With instructions like DCR, ANA, ORA, PUSH, and POP the programmer can understand what is supposed to happen when the program is run. In assembly language programming these terms are actually used to write the software and the assembler does the clerical job of translating PUSH, POP, and ORA source code into binary machine language object code. The assembler does the routine work so the programmer has more time to spend on creative aspects of the task.

STEPS IN ASSEMBLY LANGUAGE PROGRAMMING

Although each computer has its own assembler, (sometimes more than one) there are many similarities in the way most of them operate. In the remainder of this chapter we will walk through on paper the development of a short piece of software and describe the various parts of a typical assembler and their uses.

Writing and Editing Programs

Most assembler packages include some type of editor. Editors make the job of program writing much easier by providing convenient ways of typing in and modifying lines of instructions. The Editor/Assembler for the TRS-80 (Radio Shack, $29.95), is a case in point. When the program is loaded into memory it is possible to begin typing in the program you want to develop. Each line you type in is placed in a *text buffer*—a special area of RAM used to temporarily store the assembly language program while it is being written. As it is entered there are several commands that can be used to facilitate the writing:

D#

Each line of program is assigned a line number as it is entered. The command *D10* will cause line 10 to be deleted. *D10:60* deletes all the lines from 10 to 60 inclusive.

Fstring

F causes the computer to search through the text buffer until it finds the string specified after F. In the example *FMVI* the string to be found would be MVI. The term string, as used here, means a pattern of 1 to 16 characters (e.g., GOTO, A2B, ORA, HI THERE). The F command is an easy way to locate a particular instruction in a long program. In the example, FMVI would cause the first line with MVI in it to be printed on the screen. The programmer could then make any required modifications in that line.

H#   P#   T#

These three commands are used to print out all or part of the program stored in the text buffer. *H60* sends line 60 to the line-printer (H stands for hardcopy) while *P60* will cause line 60 to appear on the video screen. *H1:600* sends lines 1 through 600 to the printer. The T command works just like P except no line numbers are printed.

I#

It is often necessary to add lines to an existing program. If something must be added between lines 120 and 130, for example, the command *I125* will allow a new line to be inserted in the proper location. I is also used to enter the program initially. If *I10* is typed the computer will assign the next line of program typed (up to 128 characters) to line 10. If the command *I10,5* is issued the system will assign the first line typed to line 10 and then increment the line counter by 5. Thus when the end of line 10 is signaled by pressing the ENTER key the computer automatically prints a *15* on the left margin and waits for another line to be typed in. Automatic line numbering by an editor is a very convenient feature.

L name   W name

These two commands are used to write programs onto a cassette tape for later use and to load a program previously stored on tape back into the text buffer. The command, *W MYPRO* will record the contents of the text buffer on the tape and assign the name MYPRO to the program. If the command *L MYPRO* is issued, the computer will start the recorder motor and look for a program called MYPRO on the tape. When the computer finds it, the program will be loaded back into the text buffer.

N#,#

This command is used to renumber some or all the lines in the text buffer. N10,20 will assign the number 10 to the first line of the program in the text buffer. The next line will be assigned the number 30, the next 50, and so on. The line numbers increase by the value specified after the comma. Renumbering is sometimes necessary to clean up a program that has suffered extensive editing and thus has many oddly numbered lines inserted. Renumbering also makes room for the insertion of more program lines (e.g., lines 10 and 11 would becor e 10 and 30).

R#

R stands for replace. *R125* means you want the next line typed in to be written over and replace the original line 125.

Up arrow   Down arrow

The keys with the up arrow and the down arrow on them are used to *scroll* through the program. These commands move you forward and backward through the program. Since the screen can only display 16 lines at a time, these two commands allow you to select which 16 lines will be displayed.

E#

The E or edit command is actually a way of getting at a whole series of editing options. Thus far, the commands mentioned have all been *line oriented* — that is, they all operate on a whole line or more. E# allows the use of several *character oriented* subcommands on the line specified by the number following E. Radio Shack was very crafty in selecting their character editing subcommands. They are the same instructions that are used to edit programs in the TRS-80 Level II BASIC. Here is a summary:

C#

Instructs the computer to change a certain number of characters which follow the cursor. Suppose line 225 requires editing. Typing *E225* is a way of making line 225 appear on the screen and at the same time signal the computer that you wish to do some character-by-character editing:

225 This is the line toooo fixed.

The area of the line that requires attention is over on the right. The cursor controls on the TRS-80 can be used to move the cursor over to the point where a change is necessary. In the example above it would be necessary to move the cursor over to the first *o* in *tooo*. Then type *3C*. That tells the editor that the three characters after the cursor are to be changed. After typing *3C* it would be necessary to type *be* (don't forget the space before *be*) and the three new characters (space, b,e) will replace the three *o's* that were entered by mistake.

L

In the example above typing *L* after all the tidying up is done will cause the rest of the line to be printed out so you can see it in its new form.

225 This is the line to be fixed.

After the line is typed the cursor will return to the left margin of the screen.

H

H is short for hack. This instruction deletes any part of a line that is to the right of the cursor. If *H* had been typed instead of *L* after replacing the *o's* the result would have been:

225 This is the line to be

D#

D stands for delete. *5D* means *delete the next 5 characters to the right of the cursor.* The command does more than simply erase the characters. It does not leave blank spaces in the line where the offending characters once resided. Instead, any material to the right of the deleted characters will be moved over to fill in the empty spaces produced by the deletion.

#K

K stands for *kill*. If *2Kr* is typed, the computer will delete everything on the line up to the second occurrence of *r* in the line being edited.

#S

This *search* instruction is used to move the cursor to a particular position in the line. *5Sb* will move the cursor over to the fifth *b* on the line.

X

Moves the cursor to the end of the line. Additional material can then be typed in.

I

Once the cursor is positioned at a strategic spot in the line the command *I* can be used to insert additional characters. As each character is typed (after the I command) the original material to the right of the cursor is pushed over to make room for the characters being added.

(Shift) Up Arrow   A   Q

These commands are used to halt the editing process. When A is typed, any editing done on the line will be undone and the line will return to its original condition — nice for those colossal blunders that always seem to happen on a crucial line. After the command *A,* the cursor will move to the beginning of the line and editing can begin all over again. Q, which stands for quit, causes the computer to leave the character editing mode altogether. To continue editing another E# must be typed. And finally, if you are in the middle of a particular editing subcommand (e.g., you've typed *5Kd* but haven't pressed the ENTER key) that particular instruction can be cancelled by holding the Shift key down and pressing the up arrow key.

The line and character-oriented editing commands described above make writing assembly language programs much easier. Many people also use these editing features to write regular letters and papers. The computer doesn't care whether you're working on a program or a letter to Uncle Jim.

The Language of Assembly Language

It has already been noted that assembly language uses terms like MVI instead of binary or hex numbers. There is also a complex set of rules that must be followed in writing assembly language programs. These rules correspond to the grammar and syntax rules in English. Both can sometimes be picky and frustrating to deal with.

A typical assembly language or *source code* listing will have several components. Here is a modified version of a program used in the TRS-80 Assembler/Editor manual as an example. Assume we have used all our editing commands to write and edit the version listed below:

Line #	Label	OPCODE	OPERAND	COMMENTS
00100		ORG	5000H	
00110	VIDEO	EQU	3C00H	
00120		LD	HL,VIDEO	;SOURCE ADDRESS
00130		LD	DE,VIDEO +1	;DEST, ADDRESS
00140		LD	BC,400H	;BYTE COUNT
00150		LD	(HL),02AH	;ASCII *
00160		LDIR		;FILL SCREEN
00170	;JUMP TO BASIC WHEN B KEY IS PRESSED			
00180	KSCN	LD	A,(3801H)	;LOAD FROM KBD
00190		CP	04H	
00200		JP	NZ,KSCN	
00210		JP	0H	;RETURN TO BASIC
00220		END		

The line number on the left is just a convenient way of putting some order into the whole process. Line numbers need not be consecutive (e.g., 100, 101, 102,...) and they do not usually start at 0. It is common to start at 10 or 100 and to use increments of 5 or 10. In the sample program the increment is 10 and the program begins with line 100.

The label column is optional in the TRS-80 Assembler, but it serves a very useful purpose. In some assemblers a label is a shorthand way of indicating the function of a particular section of code. If the line containing the label is the beginning of a code conversion subroutine, for example, the label CONV might appear in the label column. Most assemblers limit labels to 5 or 6 characters and require that the label be typed with a blank space between the line number and the label. Later typing CONV would be the same as typing the memory address where CONV begins.

The TRS-80 Assembler also uses the label column a little differently. The labels in the TRS-80 listing can be *symbolic* labels. A symbolic label is a name that stands for a particular number. In line 120, for example, the symbolic label VIDEO is set to equal (EQU) the hexadecimal number 3C00, the first address of the video display RAM in the TRS-80. After line 120 it will be possible to use the symbolic label VIDEO in place of the number 3C00 hex. Typing VIDEO is the same as typing 3C00.

While the TRS-80 Assembler accepts symbolic labels it, like many assemblers, will also accept the first type of label mentioned above. Those that use both types will have specific rules that help the computer identify which type is intended.

The heart of the listing is the OPCODE column. This section contains the mnemonic codes that will actually become the program. In the example, there are three mnemonics on the first three lines (ORG, EQU, and LD). Two of these are *pseudo-ops* and the other is a standard Z-80 mnemonic. Pseudo-ops are terms the assembler understands even though they are not really translatable into machine language instructions. That is, they do not stand for a particular Z-80 instruction. The TRS-80 Assembler understands nine pseudo-ops. The three that will be used in the sample program are defined below:

ORG

When the program is assembled it will start (ORiGinate) at the address specified after ORG. In the example, line 100 tells the assembler that the program should be set up so that it begins at memory location 5000 hex. In the TRS-80, 5000H is the beginning of the user RAM area.

EQU

The number that follows EQU will be assigned to the label that precedes EQU. The label VIDEO is set to equal 3C00H in line 110. EQU creates *symbolic* labels.

END

Just like the movies. END tells the computer there is no source code beyond END to be assembled.

The three instructions used in the sample program are presented in the Z-80 instruction manual, and all assemblers include manuals which explain all the instructions and their formats. A little review here won't hurt, however. First, though, some explanation of the operand column is required. That column is used to supply the one or two values needed by some instructions. An instruction that puts data in a particular memory location, for example, must have the location specified in the operand column. If two numbers appear in the operand column they must be separated by a comma. As you will see, the values needed by an instruction can be specified by a number, a symbolic label, or by naming a register or register pair.

Now let's look at the instructions needed in our program.

LD

In line 120 the instruction *LD HL,VIDEO* appears. That translates into *load the HL register pair with the number 3C00H*. The basic format for the instruction requires the destination to be specified first in the operand column, followed by the number to be transferred. Several other variations of LD are used in the program but most work the same as the one in line 120. The one exception in line 150 will be explained later.

LDIR

This is a very complicated instruction. Its completion is a three step process. In the first step the CPU looks at the HL register pair for a memory address. It then goes to the memory address it found in HL and retrieves the number stored there. That number is put in another memory location. The second location is specified by the number stored in the DE register pair. Thus far then, we have a number transferred from one memory location to another.

The CPU then adds 1 to the DE and HL register pairs (*increments* in computer talk) and subtracts 1 from the BC register pair (decrements).

Here comes some fancy footwork now. If the BC register pair does not contain the number zero after 1 is subtracted in the second step above, the CPU decreases the program counter (PC) register by 2. Since the PC register tells the computer where the next instruction to be executed is stored, subtracting 2 from PC has the effect of starting the execution of this little song and dance all over again. The upshot of all this is that the program will keep executing this instruction until BC does equal 0. When BC reaches 0 the computer proceeds to the next instruction in the program. If BC equalled 0 in the first place, before 1 was subtracted, the program would end up executing the instruction 65536 times before BC equalled 0 again.

JP

Line 200 contains a conditional jump command. JP NZ,KSCN means *If the Z flag is not zero, jump to the address specified by the label KSCN.* If the zero flag is *0* the program continues execution with the instruction on the next line. Another jump command is shown on line 210. It is not conditional. When the program reaches *JP 0H* it will jump to address location 0 and begin executing whatever instruction is stored there.

CP

In line 190 the instruction *CP 04H* tells the computer to *compare* the contents of the A register with the number that follows, in this case 04 hex. If the number in A minus 04 hex equals 0 the Z flag is *set* equal to *1*.

Assembling the Program

After the program has been written in assembly language and corrected, the next step is to actually assemble it. In the TRS-80 Assembler this is accomplished by typing the command *A* followed by a space and the name you want to assign to the program. If the command *A FLSCRN* is given, the computer will assemble whatever is in its text buffer and name it FLSCRN. Assembling the program involves, among other things, converting assembly language terms to machine language (source code to object code), replacing labels with the actual values they represent, and checking the program for errors. When all that is done the computer will print out the assembler listing. Here is what FLSCRN would look like:

Assembled Version of FLSCRN

5000	00100	ORG	5000H
3C00	00110	EQU	3C00H
5000 21003C	00120	LD	HL,VIDEO
5003 11013C	00130	LD	DE,VIDEO+1
5006 010004	00140	LD	BC,400H
5009 362A	00150	LD	(HL),2AH

```
500B EDB0                00160              LDIR
                         00170  ;JUMP TO BASIC WHEN B KEY
                                 IS PRESSED
500D 3A0138              00180  KCSN    LD      A,3801H
5010 FE04                00190          CP      04H
5012 C20D50              00200          JP      NZ,KSCN
0000                     00210          END
00000 TOTAL ERRORS
KSCN  500D
VIDEO 3C00
READY CASSETTE
```

Note that one of the pieces of information at the bottom of the listing is the number of errors the Assembler found. When one or more errors are listed it is necessary to find and correct them before the program can actually be used. Just below the error total is the symbol table. For this program it lists the actual memory addresses of the two labels used in the program, KSCN and VIDEO.

The three columns on the right are the same as they were in the earlier listing. The two on the left, however, have been added by the assembler. The machine language object codes, in hexadecimal, appear beside their memory addresses. Since this program originates at 5000H, the first byte of the program will reside at 5000H. The rest of the program will be placed in consecutive addresses above 5000H.

Lines 100 and 110 of the assembled program contain no machine language instructions. Instead they contain specific information relating to the two pseudo-op codes used in the program. The third line begins with 5000, the memory location where the first object code, 21, will be stored. Beside 21 are two more hex numbers, 00 and 3C. That is the value which will be loaded into HL. Notice that the order has been reversed — 3C 00 has become 00 3C. The reason for the reversal takes a little explaining. A four digit hex number requires 16 bits to be written in binary. If that 16 bit binary number is actually a memory address that will be loaded into a register pair, it is necessary to load the lowest or least significant 8 bits of the address first. Then the other 8 bits (most significant) are loaded.

3C	00	hex number
00111100	00000000	binary number
Highest 8 bits	Lowest 8 bits	

Note that the letters assigned to the register pair HL reflect which 8 bits of an address will be loaded in which register. H gets the highest 8 bits of the address and L the lowest. Since the instruction loads L first, the portion of the number intended for it must be listed first.

Notice also that the memory address 5000 appears on line 120 while the next line begins with 5003. What happened to 5001 and 5002? Actually, line 120 has three 8-bit (2 digit hex) numbers (21, 00, and 3C). So 21 will be put in 5000, 00 in 5001, and 3C in 5002. Thus the first code on line 140 (11 hex) will be placed in memory location 5003.

The remainder of the listing is relatively straightforward. Below the error total on the listing is a symbol table. The symbolic labels used are listed on the left with their actual values on the right. The listing ends with the line READY CASSETTE. This assembler will record the machine language program it has created from our assembly language program when the ENTER key is pressed. If all goes well the outcome of our work will be a cassette tape which contains the machine language version. Once recorded it can be loaded into the computer and executed later. The assembler need not be in memory; the program will run independent of it.

A Walk Through of the Program

Before we wave a fond farewell to assembly language, let's go through the demonstration program line by line and find out exactly what is happening:

```
00100        ORG        5000H
```

This line uses the pseudo op code, ORG, to tell the computer where the final product, the machine language program, will originate in memory. The program will start at location 5000H. The TRS-80 Assembler accepts hex, octal, and decimal numbers. It is thus necessary to add H, O, or D after each number so the computer will know which base is being used.

```
00110        VIDEO        EQU        3C00H
```

The symbolic label, VIDEO, is set to equal 3C00H. After line 110, the symbol VIDEO will be interpreted as the number 3C00H.

00120   LD   HL,VIDEO

The number 3C00H is loaded into register pair HL.

00130   LD   DE,VIDEO + 1

The number 3C00 + 1 or 3C01H is put into register pair DE.

00140   LD   BC,400H

The number 400H is loaded into register pair BC. The number
400H is 1024 decimal. There are 1024 *locations* on the video
screen of the TRS-80 which are arranged in 16 rows with 64
locations on each row for a total of 1024 locations.

00150   LD   (HL),02AH

The instructions on this line look a lot like those on preceding
lines. The parentheses around HL, however, make it very different. The number after (HL) is loaded into the memory location specified by the number in HL. Since 3C00H is the value
currently residing in HL, 2A hex will be stored in memory location 3C00H. It happens that 3C00 is not an ordinary memory
location in the TRS-80. It is the first byte of memory that is
dedicated to the video display. The number placed in 3C00 will
be interpreted as a signal to display something in the upper left-
hand corner of the screen. Since 2A hex is the ASCII code for a
star (☆) or asterisk (*), that is exactly what will appear on the
top left of the screen when the instruction is executed.

00160   LDIR

The LDIR instruction has already been explained. In this program it will first look at HL and find 3C00. It then takes the
number stored in memory location 3C00, which is 2AH, and
stores it in the memory location specified by the number in DE.
It just so happens that DE has 3C01H, the address of the video
display memory byte adjacent to 3C00, in it. That means it controls the display location on the top line, one space over from
the left margin. Now we have a 2A in two video dislay locations.
LDIR, in its own inimical style, adds 1 to both HL and DE while

BC is decreased by 1, and the PC or program counter is reduced by 2. The LDIR instruction is a two byte instruction (ED B0) and reducing the PC by 2 means LDIR will be executed again. On the second execution the value stored in the memory location pointed to by the HL register pair (now 3C01 since HL was incremented by 1) and put it in the memory location specified by DE (now 3C02 after incrementing). This sort of piggyback pattern will continue for 1024 bytes (400H). The program will not go beyond LDIR as long as the BC register pair has a value other than 0. Since 1 is subtracted from BC each time the loop is executed, and 400H or 1024D was put in BC in line 140 the loop will be executed 1024D times before BC reaches 0. Since there are 1024 positions on the video display there will be a full screen of ☆'s before the computer proceeds to line 170 and beyond.

> 00170   ;JUMP TO BASIC WHEN B KEY IS PRESSED

Line 170 has no instruction on it, only a comment that summarizes what the following lines are supposed to do.

> 00180   KSCN   LD   A,(3801H)

The A register is loaded with the data stored in memory location 3801H. At least that is what appears to happen. Actually things are a bit more complicated in TRS-80 land. The memory address 3801 is no ordinary RAM BYTE. It is part of the keyboard decoding system of the computer. Location 3801 will contain all zeroes unless one of the following keys is pressed — @, A, B, C, D, E, F or G. If any one of these keys is pressed, one bit in the byte at 3801 will change from zero to one. If B is pressed, the byte in 3801 becomes 00000100. That equals 04 in decimal and 04 in hex. After this line, the A register will contain 8 zeroes (no key pressed) or an 8 bit binary number that has a *1* in one of the eight bits.

> 00190   CP   04H

This line compares the contents of the Accumulator with 04H. If the register contains 04H the zero flag will be *set*. The only way A will contain 04H is if the *B* key on the keyboard has been pressed.

00200   JP   NZ,KSCN

If the zero flag is not set the program will jump back to line 180 and execute the loop again. It will keep looking through these lines until the user presses B on the keyboard. That puts 04H in memory address 3801 and thus into the Accumulator. When the 04H in A is compared to 04H in line 190 it sets the zero flag, and the conditional jump in line 200 will not be executed. Until that happens, however, the conditional jump will send the computer back to KSCN which means a screen full of stars (☆) will be displayed until *B* is pressed.

00210   JP   0H

Once the program reaches line 210 the program will jump to memory address 0H. That is the starting location of BASIC. The computer will clear the screen, begin executing its BASIC interpreter, and will print out its customary greeting message on the screen.

Other assemblers will not work exactly like the one for the TRS-80, but there will usually be quite a bit of similarity. More sophisticated assemblers may add a few bells and whistles. Some offer prepackaged *macro* instructions. A macro is an instruction recognized by the assembler which actually stands for a whole group of instructions. An example of a macro would be a series of instructions that gets data from a memory location and sends it to a printer after checking to see if the printer is ready to print. A programmer who needs to include a printer subroutine can use the macro instead of actually writing out the individual op codes. When the program is assembled the assembler replaces the macro with the appropriate machine language instructions.

This chapter on assembly language programming certainly has not exhausted the topic (although I am) — there is much more to learn. It is, however, a good beginning. Readers should be able to read, understand, and use assembler listings for their computer. With careful reading of an assembler manual many of you should be able to begin writing short but useful programs and subroutines.

CHAPTER 6

Quick and Dirty BASIC

In the beginning, personal computing often involves a lot of decision making. Which chip? Which computer? Buy or build? How much memory? What peripherals? What language to learn? Let me take that last decision off your shoulders. Learn BASIC. Although it takes more memory capacity to run programs written in a higher level language like BASIC, the advantages associated with it far outweigh that disadvantages — particularly when the price of memory seems to be dropping almost daily. BASIC is easy to learn — well, at least it isn't difficult. And most of the canned programs in the magazines are written in one version of BASIC or another. There is, in fact, a mountain of BASIC software available at a nominal cost. And many manufacturers include BASIC in ROM as a standard feature. Just turn the machine on and BASIC is ready to work. In a few years we may have a new language, perhaps PASCAL for small computers, but for now learn BASIC.

BASIC was developed at Dartmouth College in 1963 by John Kemeny and Thomas Kurtz. Dr. Kemeny is now the retired president of Dartmouth College (and also chairman of the committee which investigated the Three Mile Island nuclear accident). BASIC stands for Beginners All-purpose Symbolic Instruction Code. It is a modification of ALGOL, another high level language, and is one of the easiest to learn. Since 1963 over 100 books have been written about BASIC. Most of them are good; they teach you how to write your own programs in BASIC, provided, of course, that you stick with the book long enough to learn all the material. In a way, they're like the foreign language textbooks that are used in high school and university courses. If a student does well in two or three years of training he or she can end up speaking like a native.

Most of us, however, do not want to invest the time needed to speak like a native. We just want to know enough to read a menu and tell the waiter to lay off the hot sauce. That's where the next three chapters come in. They're like a Berlitz short-course in BASIC for the tourist. You may not be able to write your own programs when you finish, but you should be able to understand someone else's programs, and make many of them run in your own computer.

When I finished building my first computer, I sat for a day or two just watching the letters magically appear on the TV screen. That won't maintain your interest for long though. My next move was to drag out all the magazines and books I had and begin selecting programs that I wanted to run. That is where I hit a major snag. There are over 40 different *versions* of BASIC. Some are standard BASICS that have all the regular instructions. The exact way these instructions are used, however, may vary slightly, from version to version. Those slight variations are often enough to keep a program written in one version from running in another. And then there are the Tiny BASICs. *Dr. Dobbs Journal* has published several of these. Actually they are not really BASICs; they are shorter, less complex languages which were modeled after BASIC. Tiny BASIC was developed for use in home computers which had very little memory capacity. To make the program fit in less than 2K of memory, many of the rarely used instructions and some of the conveniences were eliminated. Finally, there are a number of *extended* BASICs. These versions have all the commands, statements, and functions of a standard BASIC plus a number of additional features that make programming easier or more efficient.

Lack of standardization is a major drawback when someone wants to use a canned program from a book or magazine. This is especially true when the person is not a sophisticated BASIC user. Without extensive modifications, most programs that are not written in Tiny BASIC will not run in a computer that uses one of these preshrunk languages. Even with a standard BASIC it is not usually possible to simply type a program into the computer and run it unless it was originally writtin in the same version of BASIC. The first game I picked to try out on my Sol was a number guessing game called STARS. I first loaded BASIC 5, a 5K version from Processor Technology, into the computer from cassette. It worked fine. Then I began typing in the STARS program line by line. Even after I found and corrected numerous typing errors, the game would not run. It was written in Hewlett-Packard's 2000F BASIC, a very good version but one that is not completely compatible with Processor Technology's 5K BASIC. Disheartened, and not a little depressed at not being able to run even the simplest game, I made my one-hundredth trip to the computer store (I had hoped the frequency of visits would decrease once the thing was built). An experienced BASIC programmer spotted my problem immediately. The H-P version has a command that allows a letter and a dollar sign (A$) to stand for a word or string of words; PT 5K does not. It was only necessary to change two lines, and the program ran perfectly.

Whether the computer will be used for business or for fun, most beginners will want to start by doing the same thing I did — modify existing programs so they work in their computer. Writing original programs should come later. The next four chapters will provide an overview of how BASIC works, explain what the instructions mean, and provide some guidelines for making programs work in your computer. With this information you can be a consumer of programs without making the time investment required to produce your own.

GETTING ACQUAINTED

For many readers the meaning of terms like *statement, command,* and *function* is probably unclear at this point. A command is an instruction that is to be acted upon immediately. A statement, in contrast, is an instruction that is to be executed later, usually in the course of running a program. Some instructions can be treated as either commands or statements while others work only as statements. Here is an example that might clarify the point:

PRINT 5 + 6

30 PRINT 5 + 6

If the first line above were typed and the return or enter key pressed, many BASICs will immediately print the answer *11*. PRINT is used in the first line as a command because it is executed as soon as the carriage return key is pressed. The PRINT in the second line, however, is a statement since the computer will simply place it in the current program. In order to get line 30 to do its thing, it would be necessary to type RUN. That would cause the current program, of which line 30 is one part, to be executed. To summarize then, a statement is preceeded by a line number and is executed later, a command does not have a line number and is executed immediately. Commands that are found in many BASICs include LIST, RUN, CLEAR, BYE, SCRATCH, CSAVE, and CLOAD.

In general usage the term *statement* applies not only to individual instructions but to each line of instruction in a program. A *multiple statement line* would be a line in a program that contains several separate instructions:

    10 LET A = 10   (a one statement line)
    20 LET A = 10: LET B = 12   (a two statement line)

Sometimes the term *keyword* is used to identify the main word that tells the computer what to do with the rest of the line. In lines 10 and 20 the word LET is the keyword.

Now to the term *function*. Most BASICs have a variety of very useful instructions that perform a specified operation on a variable. SQR(A), for example, will produce the square root of A. A function is, in many ways, a shorthand way of performing a subroutine. Instead of writing out all the math required to take the square root of a number, compute the natural log, or obtain the tangent; it is possible to use a function instead. In addition to math functions such as those described above there are also string functions. LEN(A$) will, for example, tell you how many characters are in the string A$.

When most people buy their computer, the type of BASIC available for it gets about as much consideration as the color of the cabinet. As noted above, there are major differences between BASICs. Palo Alto Tiny BASIC, for example, will run in a little over 2K of memory, costs very little, but has only three commands, nine statements, no error messages, and no editing features. MITS 8K BASIC, on the other hand, requires over 6K of memory, and can be expensive to buy. But it has eight commands and twenty-three statements, extensive editing capabilities, and many error messages that tell the programmer what is wrong.

Being the products of human hands, the available BASICs also vary in their degree of perfection. Some, like the three

MITS versions and the Polymorphic BASIC, have good reputations for reliability. The major differences between them are related to the number of different instructions the comuputer will understand and the amount of memory required. The more memory needed, the more sophisticated the BASIC. Some versions, however, have been criticized for various reasons. As an example, the late IMSAI 8K 1.4 BASIC had a spartan instruction manual and a number of internal problems as well. Even MITS 8K is flawed for some purposes. It will not run in a computer that uses the Z-80 chip because of some programming tricks that were used when it was developed.

BASICs also differ in the amount of time they require to run a standard or *benchmark* program. Tom Rugg and Phil Feldman compared the time it took each of 31 BASICs to run a number of benchmark programs and published the results in *Kilobaud* magazine. The differences were enormous. One program, for example, took 21 seconds in one system and over 35 minutes in another!

A buyer is not likely to base the entire decision of which computer to buy on how good its BASIC is, but that should be one consideration. Since quality depends on how well the product will do what you have in mind, no specific recommendations will be made here about the *best* BASIC. And, in addition, most of the major software producers regularly come out with improved versions. When you decide to buy, check with someone who is familiar with the BASIC you will be using to be sure it is acceptable.

HOW TO USE THIS CHAPTER

It would be possible for a reader to plow through these chapters without a computer and still learn some BASIC. My advice is to wait until the computer has arrived. Then read the BASIC chapters, learn what the statements and commands mean, and use your computer to do the examples scattered through the reading. Don't, however, try to memorize definitions and instructions. Practice enough so that working in BASIC is comfortable for you, but use the chapters and the manual that comes with your BASIC as reference material. It is not necessary to be able to say off the top of your head what *GOSUB 140* means; you only need to know where to look it up. After working with BASIC for a while it will become a familiar second language through experience, not memorization.

INTRODUCTION TO BASIC

There are several important differences between the language spoken by a computer and regular English. In English the meaning will usually be clear even if a word or two is mispronounced or misspelled. BASIC and other computer languages are not so forgiving. You must say precisely what you intend to, and say it exactly as the computer expects.

Another difference is in the way punctuation is handled. Commas, semicolons, and periods clarify the meaning of written English, but the rules for their use vary. You could still understand a letter from Uncle Harry even if he managed to write a whole page without a comma or period. In BASIC these punctuation marks are often as important as the letters and numbers. Leaving out one comma can prevent an entire program from running properly.

Finally, English is a very rich language. There are usually several words that have similar meanings. A 1956 Chevrolet could appropriately be called a car, auto, automobile, or vehicle. BASIC is not so well endowed. There is often only one way of saying something. The words BASIC understands are called *key words*.

To make the computer do something, these key words are used to make up STATEMENTS. Statements correspond to sentences in English. Note that this definition of the term "statement" is different from the one given earlier. Three examples of statements are given below:

```
10 LET A = 2
20 LET B = 4
30 PRINT A + B
RUN
```

Each statement is preceded by a line number. When a computer is told to RUN a program it begins with the statement that has the lowest line number and follows the instructions given in that statement. It then proceeds through the program until all the statements have been acted upon. When it reaches line 30 it would do the arithmetic requested $(2+4)$ and print the results. Follow the instructions given with your computer and load BASIC. Then see if the example program will work. Some computers require BASIC to be loaded from cassette tape; others put it on a disk, and still others put BASIC in ROM so that it is available for use as soon as the computer is switched on.

The three statements make up a simple PROGRAM. A program is a set of instructions or statements that tell the computer how to solve a particular problem. To load a program into the computer, type in each statement beginning with its line number and ending with a carriage return (Sometimes the key is labeled *RETURN* or *ENTER*.) When the three-statement program is loaded, type RUN and hit carriage return. If the computer responds by printing 6 you are off and running.

Some Details

One of the best ways to learn about BASIC is to actually use it to do something useful, and in the rest of this chapter we'll do just that. The first of our training programs is listed in TABLE 6-1. It is a simplified version of a popular short program that should run in most BASICs. For convenience, long lines such as 10 and 20 have been divided in Table 6-1. When you type in the program on your computer avoid splitting lines such as 10 and 20. Just type in the entire line and hit the ENTER or RETURN key when you're finished.

Table 6-1

```
LIST
  10  PRINT "THIS PROGRAM COMPUTES THE
      TOTAL AMOUNT OF MONEY"
  20  PRINT "YOU WILL ACCUMULATE IF YOU
      SAVE A SPECIFIED AMOUNT"
  30  PRINT "EACH YEAR."
  40  PRINT
  50  PRINT "HOW MANY DOLLARS WILL YOU
      INVEST YEARLY?"
  60  INPUT A
  70  PRINT "FOR HOW MANY YEARS WILL
      YOU INVEST?"
  80  INPUT N
```

```
 90   PRINT "WHAT RATE OF INTEREST WILL
      YOU RECEIVE?"
110   INPUT R
115   LET R = R/100
120   PRINT
130   PRINT "YEAR", "TOTAL INVEST", "", "TTL.
      ACCUMULATED"
140   PRINT
150   LET B = 1 + R
155   PRINT 1,A, "",A
160   FOR L = 1 TO N
170   LET B = B*(1 + R)
180   LET S = (A*(B – 1))/R
190   IF L<N THEN PRINT L + 1,(L + 1)*A,"",S
200   NEXT L
```

Table 6-1A.

If your BASIC refuses to run the program as shown in Table 6-1 substitute the following for lines 190 to 200:

```
190   IF L<N THEN 192
191   GOTO 200
192   PRINT L + 1,(L + 1)*A,"",S
200   NEXT L
```

The substitutions above will allow the program to run on a computer (e.g., Exidy's Sorcerer) whose BASIC expects to see a line number after THEN.

I will assume that your input/output system is either a Teletype or a keyboard/CRT screen and that you know how to turn on the system and load BASIC. Most BASICs will give some signal that they are ready by printing the word *READY* or *OK*. When you get that far, begin by typing in the statements for the first program exactly as listed in Table 1. A Teletype only has uppercase letters, but if you have a system that provides lowercase as well, find the switch or key that sets it for uppercase only. Be sure to type the program exactly as shown. Remember to include any final punctuation marks at the end of a line and insure that the sequence of letters, numbers and punctuation marks is copied exactly. Beginning programmers also tend to use the *l* when they really want the numeral *l* and to use a capital

O instead of the number zero (Ø). The computer is very strict when it comes to things like this. It can give only one meaning to each of the codes it receives from the keyboard. To help distinguish the letter *O* from the number zero, many video displays and printers use the symbol "Ø" for zero.

Now, unless you are a better typist than I am, there will be several typing errors before all 21 lines are done. Again, read the manuals for your computer and its version of BASIC to determine whether there are sophisticated ways of correcting mistakes. Most systems, however, have at least two ways of correcting errors. Let's say you typed line 115 like this:

$$115 \quad R = R?100$$

If the mistake is discovered before hitting a carriage return and going on to the next line it is usually possible to delete as many letters as needed by pressing the delete key. Each time that key is pressed the letter to the left of the CURSOR (the marker that tells you where you're typing) will be erased. Delete keys vary from system to system. Some systems require you to press the shift key and hit 0, while others want the control and underline keys pressed.

If there are so many mistakes on a line that you would just as soon forget it and start over, press the return key and begin again using the same line number. The computer will erase the old line and replace it with the new one you type. If you find you have a line in the program that should be deleted without being replaced with another, just type its number and hit return. The line will not appear in the next listing of the program at all. If things get so bad you want to erase everything you've done and start from scratch, there is usually a command that will erase the entire program. Try the words NEW, SCRATCH, and CLEAR. Simply type one of them and press the carriage return. One of these should work. Before running the savings program, let's look at some frequently used commands.

Job Control Commands

There are four sets of commands that can be used to get the computer to manage its work. They are listed below with a description of their function.

HELLO and BYE

Typing HELLO tells the computer that a friend has come to play. It is like a knock at your door, but most of the BASICs you will use do not require it; many, in fact, will not understand it at all. BYE, however, is a frequently used command. It allows you to stop operating in BASIC and to speak directly to the computer. You might, for example, want to change the output of the computer so that it is printed rather than appearing on the screen. Typing BYE allows you to do that without destroying the material you've written in BASIC. When you are ready to work in BASIC again there may be a special command that causes the computer to RUN BASIC or it may be necessary to tell the computer where to begin executing the BASIC program, EXØ, for example, instructs several computers to begin at Ø in memory. Thus typing EXØ will put you back in BASIC if your BASIC begins at Ø in memory.

NEW and OLD

As mentioned before, NEW, or its equivalent, will erase what you've typed into memory. OLD, if your system has it, does just the reverse. It lets you continue working on a program that was already in the computer.

LIST and RUN

If you have successfully put the demonstration program *Growth of Savings* into memory, type LIST (on a separate line) and hit RETURN. The program should be printed out just as it was typed with two exceptions. Lines between 160 and 200 may be indented because they are inside a *FOR-NEXT Loop,* and the listing should appear in numerical order beginning with the smallest line number and ending with the highest. LIST just lets you see what the current version of the program looks like.

Once you are sure the program is correct, type RUN. When given a RUN command the computer will read the first statement, follow the directions given, and move on to the next line. A sample run of the Savings Program you're working on is shown in Table 6-2. The computer will print out all the material inside the quotation marks on lines 10 through 90. But at lines 60, 80 and 110 it stops and waits for the operator to give it a number. Then it takes a number, performs some computations,

Table 6-2

RUN

THIS PROGRAM COMPUTES THE TOTAL AMOUNT OF
MONEY YOU WILL ACCUMULATE IF YOU SAVE A
SPECIFIED AMOUNT EACH YEAR.

HOW MANY DOLLARS WILL YOU INVEST YEARLY
?600

FOR HOW MANY YEARS WILL YOU INVEST
?10

WHAT RATE OF INTEREST WILL YOU RECEIVE
?9

YEAR	TOTAL INVEST	TOTAL ACCUMULATED
1	600	600
2	1200	1254
3	1800	1966.86
4	2400	2743.8773
5	3000	3590.826
6	3600	4514.0006
7	4200	5520.2606
8	4800	6617.084
9	5400	7812.6213
10	6000	9115.7573

and prints out the results in an orderly little table. Try your version several times with different numbers. Each time you want
the computer to go through the program again just type RUN
and hit return. Run the program once with exactly the same information given in the sample run and check to see that your
data is the same. The computer we used gives answers of up to
four decimal places in accuracy. Yours may give more or less,
but the actual dollar value in the third column should be essentially the same. If not, check the program for errors.

SAVE and GET — Most systems have some means of preserving or destroying programs. Radio Shack or TRS-80 BASIC, for example, uses the command CSAVE to instruct the computer to record the program on a cassette. The way this is done varies so much, however, that it is probably best to consult your manual. The same goes for moving a program from tape or disk into memory. GET, LOAD and CLOAD are all used in one or more BASICs. Since the savings program will be used again later, why not save it on disk or a cassette now?

ESCAPE — A computer will occasionally take exception to something a programmer says and get upset. The cursor may disappear from the screen while it pouts, refusing to talk. Or it may begin to print something on the screen over and over with the apparent intention of making it a lifetime habit. If all else fails you can unplug the thing and start again. There is usually a less drastic alternative though. Pressing the ESCAPE or Mode Select key, the uppercase and repeat keys, or the control and C keys will often improve relations although the current program may be erased in the process. Some computers have a special BREAK key that halts execution.

Clerical Instructions

Now that you've gotten the hang of it we'll pick up the pace of things a bit. In the following sections most of the standard statements and commands of BASIC will be presented and explained. Generally the explanation will be associated with a demonstration program like the one in Table 6-1. Read the short descriptions of the BASIC instructions, then run the programs to see how they actually work.

PRINT

This statement causes the computer to print out or display whatever follows PRINT. In line 10 of the savings program, it caused a sentence to be printed. If material is enclosed in quotation marks the computer will print it exactly as typed. The material inside the quotation marks is called a STRING or a literal string. If no quotation marks are used, the computer behaves a little differently. Look at line 155 in the Growth program:

155 PRINT 1, A, " ", A

When the computer comes to this line it will not print the letter A. Instead it prints the numerical value currently assigned to A. In line 60, A is defined as the amount of money you plan to invest each year. In the run shown in this book, A was set at $600 — the amount which will be printed twice when line 155 is executed.

There is one other way to use a PRINT statement. Lines 40, 120, and 140 have a PRINT statement but nothing else. This causes the computer to insert a blank line or space so that the output can be easily read.

A final word about the PRINT statement. In some BASICs the question mark (?) at the beginning of a line is equivalent to the word PRINT. When the program is listed, the question marks are automatically converted to PRINT statements. In a long program with many PRINT statements using the "?" can save time.

Variables and Strings

A = 600

The A in the expression $A = 600$ is called a VARIABLE. Another word that would fit is "label." The 600 is the VALUE of the VARIABLE A. Look through the program in Table 6-1 and find all the variables it uses. There are six, and although all six variables used in this program are identified by a single letter, it is usually permissible to designate a variable in several other ways. If there are many variables in a program they can be identified by two symbols — a letter and another letter, number or symbol (e.g., AB,M3,R&). There is one limitation, however, to the way names are given to variables. Many BASICs only need the first two letters of a command or statement to operate. That means PR is the same as PRINT. Thus, variable names can be any two character combination that is not already used by the computer for some other purpose.

Did you find the six variables? There is A in line 60, N in line 80, R in 110, B in 150, L in 160, and S in 180. (L is a special case that will be discussed later). Each variable also has a VALUE assigned to it. The value can be a number ($A = 600$), another variable ($X = A$, for example), or a mathematical expression like

$(B = B*(1 + R))$. The asterisk (*) is the computer's way of indicating multiplication. Thus B equals "B times the sum of one plus R." Note also that the value of a variable can be modified at different points in a program. In the Savings Program, R is input into the system as a whole number (e.g., 9), but it is changed from a percent to a decimal in line 115 so it can be conveniently used in the formulas.

Commas and Semicolons

The importance of quotation marks has already been mentioned. Two other frequently used punctuation marks are the comma and the semicolon. Look closely at Line 30:

130 Print "Year", "Total Invest", " ", "TTL Accumulated"

There are four strings in this PRINT statement. Three of them have words in their string while one has only a space. The strings are separated by commas. Those commas are important. In BASIC the comma works a little like the tab function on a typewriter. Inserting a comma causes the material following it to be placed at one of four predefined places across the screen. In our program, Line 130 instructs the computer to print the word YEAR on the left hand margin and then move over to the second print position and write TOTAL INVEST. By next typing a vacant string (" ") we, in a way, fooled the computer into thinking there was something that was to go in the third position. Actually, it printed a blank space and moved over to the fourth position to print TTL ACCUMULATED. The comma is a handy way of lining up columns in tables. In order to get Line 190 to place $L + 1$, $1*A$, and S just beneath the headings set up in Line 130, it was only necessary to use the comma between each of the variables. The computer does the rest. Note how 190 gets S to appear under TTL ACCUMULATED by using two commas in a row.

But what if you don't want your material spread out all across the screen? Try this with your program. Go back and replace Line 130 with a new one. This time type it exactly the same except use semicolons instead of commas. Then run the program. Now instead of being spread out, all the words are placed right next to each other. There may not even be a space between them. When a semicolon is used, it is necessary to include any spaces that are necessary inside the quotation marks (e.g., "YEAR ").

Notice that there are no commas or semicolons at the end of statements. Some BASICs will supress a normal carriage return when the , or ; appears at the end of a statement. The computer will then print whatever comes next on the same line. Change line 50 to the following:

> 50 PRINT "HOW MANY DOLLARS WILL YOU
> INVEST YEARLY?";

If you're using one of the more sophisticated BASICs, it may print a question mark right after the question and wait for a number input to be entered on the same line.

The Colon (:) and REMARK

Some programs have a large number of short lines that are tedious to type, especially when each short statement must be given a different line number. Some of the tedium can be avoided by putting more than one statement on a line. Some BASICs allow this through the use of the : (or the \). Lines 150 and 155 could be rewritten as shown below on one line:

> 150 LET B = 1 + R: PRINT 1,A,"",A

There are a few restrictions on the use of the colon. DATA statements must be put on a line by themselves, and GOTO as well as REMARK statements must be the last thing on a multiple statement line. The terms DATA and GOTO will be covered later. The REMARK statement is a way of putting a note to yourself in the program without affecting what the computer does. REMARK statements are ignored when the program is run, but they do appear when a LIST command is given. If you can afford the memory space they take up, the liberal use of REMARK statements to explain what each part of a program does can be very helpful, especially when modifications or corrections are made.

Math Expressions

BASIC uses the regular symbols to indicate addition (+) and subtraction (−). Multiplication is indicated by an asterisk (*)

and division by a slash (/). The expressions

$$A = 5*4 + 1 : B = 20/4 - 1$$

means "A equals five times four plus one" and "B equals twenty divided by four minus one." The variable A thus equals 21 and B equals 4. There is one more math symbol that is frequently seen in programs. Look at the two examples below:

$$R = 5*5*5 \qquad\qquad R = 5\uparrow3$$

Both these expressions equal 125. The first uses a series of multiplication symbols to obtain the answer. The second expression is read as "Five raised to the third power" or "Five cubed." The symbol for that is the up arrow (↑) on most computers.

When BASIC is instructed to do a series of math operations it follows a standard sequence in doing them. All the power computations are done first, then the multiplication and division is finished. Finally, the addition and subtraction is computed. A handy mnemonic to remember the standard sequence is "Please, My Dear Aunt Sally", for Power, Multiply, Divide, Add, and Subtract. When there are several of the same types of math to be done, the computer will do the work on the left first and then work across to the right.

Sometimes the standard order of computing is not the one needed to solve a problem. It can be changed by the use of parentheses. The computer will do all the computations inside parentheses, regardless of its type, before it does the work outside the parentheses. Consider the two expressions below:

$$B = 6*4 - 3 \qquad\qquad B = 6*(4 - 3)$$

B equals 21 in the first expression because the multiplication is done first. Then the three is subtracted from the result. B equals 6 in the second expression because the subtraction is done first, then the multiplication. Line 180 in the sample program given earlier shows the use of two sets of parentheses to control the order of computation. The computer will do everything inside the inner-most set of parentheses first, then work in the next, and finally do the work outside both. When using parentheses,

always be sure to give one right parenthesis for every left parenthesis, otherwise the computer will stop work and print an error
message.

Getting Information into the Computer

There are three major ways BASIC allows the programmer to
tell the computer what values are to be assigned to each
variable: the LET statement, the INPUT statement, and the
READ-DATA statements.

LET

The Savings Program example used four LET statements to
assign values to variables. Each of them is an example of LET in
one of its simpler versions. All LET does is tell the computer
that from now on a particular variable (e.g., A) will have a certain value (e.g., 25.7). In the sample program the variable R was
initially given a value by an INPUT statement. Then in line 115
it was given another value by a LET statement. Redefining
variables is an acceptable and, in fact, desirable programming
technique. As the computer moves down the program it will
consider a variable to have the value that was assigned to it last.

Now for some of the finer points of LET. Most BASICs do
not require you to actually write out the word LET. So, instead
of typing LET $B = 1 + R$ in line 150, you need only type in
$B = 1 + R$, and the LET is understood. Many versions also allow
the use of a LET statement to assign a string value to a variable.
Here is an example:

220 LET A$ = "GREAT! YOU GOT THAT ONE RIGHT."

The dollar sign attached to the A indicates it is a string variable;
that is, a variable made up of letters and symbols but having no
particular numerical or mathematical qualities. Now if you tell
the computer to PRINT A$ it will print the string that is on the
right of the equal sign. In a program that uses the same word or
sentence over and over, it saves time to be able to type the
variable name (A$) in place of the entire string.

Thus far, the names of variables have been either a single letter or a letter and a dollar sign (for string variables). For

variables with numerical values you can also use double letter names (AB, XZ, etc.), a letter and a number (U2, H0, T4), or a letter and a symbol (Q%, B#, F&). Keep in mind that any two letter combination is acceptable except for those combinations that are the beginning of a command or statement. You could not, for example, name a variable PR or LE since those letter combinations are the beginning of PRINT and LET.

A final point. The value assigned to a variable can be a number (LET A = 7), but it can also be another variable (LET A = J), or a value that must be computed (LET A = J + 7/21).

INPUT

When the computer comes to an INPUT statement it stops and waits for the operator to provide it with some data. For most variables (A, B, A1, etc.) the computer stops and waits for a number to be input. If the variable to be given a value ends in a dollar sign ($) the computer will expect a string. If the string will need spaces, it is usually necessary to enclose the string in quotation marks and put the spaces needed inside the quotation marks. When the string is printed the quotation marks will not appear, but the spaces will.

READ DATA

There are no READ or DATA statements in the Savings Program. The use of READ and DATA will be illustrated with a short program on temperature conversion.

Table 6-3

```
10 PRINT "THIS IS A PROGRAM TO CONVERT
   FAHRENHEIT"
20 PRINT "TEMPERATURES TO CENTIGRADE"
30 READ F
40 LET C = (F – 32)*(5/9)
50 PRINT "F = F";F,"C = ";C
60 GOTO 30
70 DATA 5,10,15,20,25,30,32,35,40,45,50,55,60
80 DATA 65,70,72,80,85,90,95,100
90 END
```

Clear the computer and begin typing in the temperature program. "Clear" means erase the current program from memory (e.g., by typing NEW, SCRATCH or some other command).

Once the program is in memory, tell the computer to LIST it and check for errors. When everything appears normal, run the program. The output should look like the run shown in Table 6-4.

Table 6-4

RUN

F = 5	C = − 15
F = 10	C = − 12.2222
F = 15	C = − 9.44445
F = 20	C = − 6.66667
F = 25	C = − 3.88889
F = 30	C = − 1.11111
F = 32	C = 0
F = 35	C = 1.66667
F = 40	C = 4.44445
F = 45	C = 7.22222
F = 50	C = 10
F = 55	C = 12.7778
F = 60	C = 15.5556
F = 65	C = 18.3333
F = 70	C = 21.1111
F = 72	C = 22.2222
F = 80	C = 26.6667
F = 85	C = 29.4444
F = 90	C = 32.2222
F = 95	C = 35
F = 100	C = 37.7778

When the computer comes to a READ statement it looks for the first DATA statement. Then it takes the first item from that line and assigns it to the first variable in the READ statement. If there are several variables in the read statement (e.g., READ A,B,C), the computer will take values from the DATA line and assign them sequentially to the variables. READ and DATA always go together. There are two DATA statements in the temperature program. When the computer ran out of data in

the first statement it automatically went to the next DATA
statement.

It is also possible to have several READ statements in a program. When this happens values are assigned sequentially, that
is, the computer will not begin with the first value in the DATA
statement each time a READ statement is found. Instead it uses
each value only once. If, however, you tell the computer to read
A in the beginning of the program and then tell it later to READ
A again, it will select a new value from the DATA line. Put
more variables in the READ statements than values in the
DATA statements and most BASICs will give an error message.
That just tells the user that the program is out of data and cannot continue. Data statements are particularly useful when the
values will change from one run to another. All you need to do
is enter new DATA lines instead of retyping the whole program.

Like LET and INPUT, READ and DATA can be used with
strings as well as numbers (but not variables, math operations,
other functions, or fractions). If the variable in the READ statement is a string, its name should be a letter and a dollar sign
(e.g., READ Y$). The computer will then expect to get a string
from the DATA line. It is also possible to mix numbers and
strings in a READ statement (e.g., READ Y$, B, D, P$) but
care must be taken to insure that the DATA statement provides
the values in the proper order (e.g., DATA TAXES, 55, 34,
PROFITS). Items in a DATA statement are separated by commas, and, as in any other part of BASIC, you cannot put commas in long numbers to make them more readable. The computer will think it is dealing with several values instead of one
(e.g., 1000 not 1,000). Commas should not be placed at the end
of a DATA statement either. A string can be surrounded by
quotation marks if desired. They are, in fact, necessary if spaces
are required at either end of the string.

GOTO

The temperature program has a GOTO statement in line 60.
It tells the computer to suspend its normal practice of working
through a program sequentially and proceed to the line
specified. It is used to create LOOPS, sequences of instructions
that are used over and over. Using the GOTO statement allowed
us to write the formula for converting to centigrade and the in-

structions for printing out the results only once, and then to use them over and over with a different temperature each time.

At this point you've made quite a bit of progress toward learning to use the new language—BASIC. The next chapter will complete this introduction to the language.

CHAPTER 7

More Dirt

MAKING DECISIONS AND COMPARISONS

BASIC has several ways of comparing one variable to another and of making decisions. The most important of these are IF THEN, GOSUB, ON GOTO, and FOR NEXT.

IF THEN

Did you save the savings program? If you did, load it into the computer. It has an example of an IF THEN statement in line 190.

190 IF L<N THEN PRINT L + 1,(L + 1)*A,"",S

IF THEN is more like a family of instructions than just one statement. In line 190 the IF THEN is used to make a decision about whether the results of the data analysis should be printed. IF L is less than (<) N, THEN the computer will print several pieces of information. The IF in this statement is used to specify a "condition." If that condition is true the action specified in the THEN part is performed. There are several types of IF THEN statements.

The IF THEN statement can involve any combination of the conditions and actions listed, and it can make comparisons that involve values (IF S = 5), variables (IF X = G), strings (IF P$ = "YES"), or expressions (IF X/B = Z/A). When the condition is true the computer will proceed across the line and take whatever action is specified. If the condition is false the computer moves on to the next line in the program without taking

IF _____   THEN _____

The Condition   The Action

$<$ less than   GOTO

$>$ greater than   PRINT

$=$ equals   LET

$<=$ less than or equal   INPUT

$>=$ greater than or equal   READ

$<>$ not equal   GOSUB

                                   RETURN

                                   STOP or END

the action called for in the IF THEN statement. IF THEN allows a programmer to perform CONDITIONAL BRANCH-ING. That is, the computer will do something if and only if certain conditions exist.

FOR NEXT

Just above the IF THEN statement in our demonstration program is one of my favorite statements. Lines 170 to 190 define a LOOP. It is the heart of the program since it computes the amount of money that will be earned and prints the results. It is called a loop because it is used several times, once for each year you plan to invest. The FOR NEXT statement is used to control how many times the computer moves through the loop. Lines 170 to 200 are printed below for those of you who lost the original program and are sick of turning back to the listing in the book:

```
160  FOR  L = 1 to N
170         B = B*(1 + R)
180         S = (A*(B - 1))/R
190         IF L<N THEN PRINT L + 1,(L + 1)*A,"",S
200 NEXT L
```

The three lines between FOR and NEXT are indented automatically by some computers whether you indent them or not. It is one way to remind the programmer that he or she has created a loop that will be run through several times. The NEXT defines the lower boundary of the loop. When the computer comes to a NEXT it returns to the line where FOR occurs and goes through the loop again. The way FOR operates is a little complicated. In this case L is the "control" variable in the loop. (There is no special significance to the label L, it could be any other acceptable variable name). The expression on the other side of the equal sign tells the computer where to start and how many times to run through the loop. Line 160 says "Set L equal to 1 (the initial value for the first loop. Each time the computer runs through the loop, increase the value of L by one. When L is equal to N (the final value), go through the loop one more time and move on to the line immediately after the NEXT statement." N is the number of years you plan to invest your money, so there will be one line of results for each year you invest.

As usual there are a few fine points that have not been covered yet. Look at the FOR NEXT loop below:

```
10   PRINT "HOW MUCH MONEY DO YOU
     WANT TO INVEST"
20   PRINT "FOR FIVE YEARS?"
30   INPUT M
40   PRINT "INTEREST RATE", "PRINCIPLE
     AND INTEREST"
50   FOR = 7 to 12 STEP .5
60        R = M*(1 + I/100)Λ5
70        PRINT I,R
80   NEXT I
```

There is a new twist to this one. In its standard form, the control variable in a FOR NEXT loop will be incremented by one each time the loop is used. This program, however, is designed to print information on how much money will be earned if a certain amount of money (M) is invested for five years at several different interest rates. We do not want the loop to increase the interest (I) by one each time. A more detailed breakdown is required. By adding the comment "STEP .5" it is possible to tell the computer to increase I by only .5 rather than one. A run of the program will illustrate what happens. Replace the .5 with a 2 and the printout would begin with an interest rate of 7 percent and then give data for rates of 9 and 11 percent. Now what if you replace line 50 with this one:

50 FOR I = 12 to 7 STEP -.5

A run of this variation shows what happens. The interest rate is set initially at twelve, and each time the loop is used the rate is reduced by .5 until the final value of 7 is reached.

Table 7-1   Run of Investment Program with STEP .5

HOW MUCH MONEY DO YOU WANT TO INVEST FOR 5 YEARS
?1000

INTEREST RATE	PRINCIPAL AND INTEREST
7	1402.55
7.5	1435.63
8	1469.33
8.5	1503.66
9	1538.62
9.5	1574.24
10	1610.51
10.5	1647.45
11	1685.06
11.5	1723.35
12	1762.34

Another common variation of FOR NEXT loops is to put one inside another. The details of how this works is given in most books on BASIC. If you are using a program that has "nested loops" the main thing to remember is to be sure the NEXT statements are in the proper order. In essence, a loop inside another loop will run through its entire range every time the outside loop runs through one step.

Table 7-2   Run of Investment Program with STEP -.5

HOW MUCH MONEY DO YOU WANT TO INVEST FOR 5
YEARS
?1000

INVESTMENT RATE	PRINCIPAL AND INTEREST
12	1762.34
11.5	1723.35
11	1685.06
10.5	1647.45
10	1610.51
9.5	1574.24
9	1538.62
8.5	1503.66
8	1469.33
7.5	1435.63
7	1402.55

GOSUB RETURN

With all the money you've made following the two investment
programs that have been used as examples you're bound to need
a vacation. The next demonstration program (Table 7-3) will
provide practice loosing some of that money just in case you
end up in Atlantic City or Las Vegas. It is a game program,
Blackjack. This version is a fairly simple one that does not include fancy routines such as a running record of your earnings
or the opportunity to play by Las Vegas rules. It is still an enjoy-
able program to play, and it shows just how the next few instructions work. Don't spend too much time playing Blackjack
though, there is still a lot to be covered. This program needs
over 8K of memory if you are using a 5K BASIC that is stored in
RAM, more if the BASIC itself takes up more memory. A computer that is short on memory space may be able to run the program anyway if the instructions are omitted. Just begin at line
190 and save the memory space that would be used for the instructions. Leaving out the instructions does not affect the
operation of the program.

The Blackjack program has several new terms in it and a new
type of program component as well. Lines 500 to 590 are a SUB-

ROUTINE. A subroutine is a group of lines that serve a specialized purpose in a program. They may be used several times during a run. The subroutine between 500 and 590 selects at random a "card" which will be dealt. At line 200 the words "PLAYER HOLDS" will be printed out along with several spaces. The comma after the the quotation marks means the next string or number to be printed will be placed a little further over on the same line. Line 210 tells the computer to go to line 500 and run through the subroutine that begins there. Line 500 and those that follow it will be processed until a RETURN is encountered. When that happens the computer goes back to the line just after the GOSUB, in this case 215. The statement "GOSUB 500" appears again in line 280. This time the subroutine is used to generate a card for the dealer.

Table 7-3.

```
 10  PRINT "DIRTY BASIC BLACKJACK"
 20  PRINT "WELCOME TO THE GAME OF BLACK-
     JACK"
 30  PRINT "IF YOU NEED INSTRUCTIONS PRESS 1
     AND THE RETURN"
 40  PRINT "OR ENTER KEY. TO SKIP THE IN-
     STRUCTIONS PRESS 2 AND"
 50  PRINT "THE RETURN KEY."
 60  INPUT Z
 70  IF Z<>1 GOTO 190
 80  PRINT "WHEN THE GAME BEGINS TWO
     HANDS ARE DEALT. ONE FOR"
 90  PRINT "THE DEALER AND ONE FOR YOU.
     WHEN 'HIT?' APPEARS ON"
100  PRINT "THE SCREEN YOU MAY TAKE
     ANOTHER CARD BY PRESSING 1"
110  PRINT "AND THEN THE RETURN KEY. IF NO
     CARDS ARE NEEDED"
120  PRINT "PRESS 2 AND THEN RETURN. NEW
     HANDS ARE DEALT"
130  PRINT "AUTOMATICALLY. NOTE: AN ACE IS
     ALWAYS GIVEN A"
140  PRINT "VALUE OF ONE. YOU CANNOT
     CHOOSE BETWEEN ONE AND"
```

```
150  PRINT "ELEVEN AS IN OTHER FORMS OF
     BLACKJACK."
190  PRINT
195  PRINT
200  PRINT "PLAYER HOLDS",
210  GOSUB 500
215  C = B
250  PRINT " FOR ";B
255  PRINT " "
260  PRINT "DEALER SHOWS",
270  LET M = RND(1)*12
275  LET M = INT(M) + 1
280  GOSUB 500
290  D = B
300  PRINT " "
310  LET X = C
315  PRINT " "
320  PRINT "PLAYER";
330  GOSUB 700
335  PRINT " "
340  PRINT "DEALER'S DOWN CARD IS";
350  B = M
360  GOSUB 520
370  LET D = B + D
380  PRINT " FOR ";D
390  IF D>17 THEN 440
400  PRINT "DEALER HIT = ";
410  GOSUB 500
430  GOTO 370
440  IF D>21 THEN PRINT "DEALER BUSTS,
     PLAYER WINS"
450  IF D<22 THEN 470
460  GOTO 190
470  IF D<X THEN PRINT "DEALER WINS, PAY UP"
480  IF D>X THEN PRINT "YOU WIN THIS TIME"
490  IF D = X THEN PRINT "TIE, DEALER TAKES
     POT"
495  GOTO 190
500  LET A = RND(1)*12
505  LET B = INT(A) + 1
520  IF B = 12 THEN PRINT " K",
```

```
540  IF B = 11 THEN PRINT " 0",
550  IF B = 10 THEN PRINT " J",
570  IF B<10 THEN PRINT B,
580  IF B>10 THEN PRINT B = 10
590  RETURN
700  PRINT "HIT";
710  INPUT N
720  IF N<>1 THEN 800
730  PRINT "HIT";
740  GOSUB 500
750  LET X = X + B
760  PRINT "FOR ";X
770  IF X<22 THEN 700
780  PRINT "***********BUSTED***********"
790  GOTO 190
800  RETURN
```

EXAMPLE
DIRTY BASIC BLACKJACK
WELCOME TO THE GAME OF BLACKJACK
IF YOU NEED INSTRUCTIONS PRESS 1 AND THE
RETURN OR ENTER KEY. TO SKIP THE INSTRUC-
TIONS PRESS 2 AND THE RETURN KEY.
?2

PLAYER HOLDS   7   FOR   7

DEALER SHOWS   J

PLAYER HIT   ?   1
HIT   6   FOR   13
HIT   ?   2

DEALER'S DOWN CARD IS   1   FOR 11
DEALER HIT =   5   FOR 16
DEALER HIT =   K   FOR 26
DEALER BUSTS, PLAYER WINS

   Although a RETURN must be placed at the end of a subroutine to direct the computer to return to the line just after the
GOSUB statement, it is not necessary to go straight through the

entire subroutine every time. Another subroutine begins on 700, for example, and ends on line 800. If certain conditions are met at line 720 it will skip the rest of the routine. At line 740 it jumps over to the other subroutine to "deal a card" then returns to line 750 and contines on with the 700 to 800 subroutine. Before going further it would be a good idea to go through the Blackjack program carefully so that you understand clearly how it works. Two terms (RND and INT) may be unfamiliar. They will be explained a little later.

ON GOTO

The IF THEN statement that was discussed earlier is a useful way of allowing the computer to make a decision about whether a particular action is to be taken. IF THEN is limited by the fact that it can only be used to make a yes-no type of decision. If a particular condition is true then a direction is followed; otherwise the normal progression from one line to another occurs. ON GOTO is a way of dealing with more complicated decisions. Here is an example:

40 ON T GOTO 45, 50, 55, 60, 65

If T is 1 the computer will go to line 45, if T is 2 line 50 will be the next one processed and so on. The number of lines specified as options in an ON GOTO statement is limited only by the length of the line. In some BASICs you can keep putting numbers in until you run out of space. The value of T then determines which line is processed next. If T is zero, a negative value, or if it is larger than the number of lines listed, then the computer will simply go on to the next line after 40.

Some BASICs have a similar statement, ON GOSUB, which is used to conditionally branch into one of a number of subroutines.

SUBSCRIPTED VARIABLES

We now come to one of the last major concepts in BASIC, subscripted variables. As noted earlier, VARIABLES have names (A,A4,A$,AA, etc.), and they have values. There is another common type of variable in many BASIC programs. The variable A(4) is different from A4. A4 is simply a convenient name. A(4) on the other hand is a SUBSCRIPTED VARIABLE with A being the variable name and 4 being the subscript. If you think of the data in a computer as being a parade then A4 might be one lone clown who marches by. A(4), on the other hand, could be one of several floats that come by in a set. The float in front of A(4) is A(3) while the one following is A(5). If these floats were data in a computer they would be called a LIST or ONE DIMENSIONAL ARRAY since they go by one at a time in a single line.

Now suppose a band comes marching by. Instead of one long column, a band is made up of a MATRIX or ARRAY of people arranged in rows and columns. The person in the first row and first column might be given the variable name B (0,0) while a tuba player in the fifth row and eighth column would be B(4,7). The numbers in parentheses are one less than the actual row and column placement because we began with zero instead of one in assigning names to rows and columns. To the computer, the DOUBLE SUBSCRIPTS in the variable names for the band represent the column and row placement of the variables. This is a handy device when you have to deal with a large number of variables that are related to one another in some systematic way. It is important, however, to keep in mind that a subscripted variable such as A(2) is an entirely different variable from A2, and A$(2). A$(2) is, of course, a string variable with a single subscript. When used in a program, array subscript values can be indicated normally with a number, A(6), with a variable name, A(S), or with a calculation, A(2*B).

In many versions of BASIC, when the computer first encounters a subscripted variable it expects the subscript numbers to be between 0 and 10. Thus, if you have a set of data that is more than eleven columns wide or has more than eleven rows, the computer will probably print out an error message. This can be overridden, however, by using the DIM statement. An example will help:

40 DIM N$(20)

Line 40 tells the computer to expect the variable N$ to be a subscripted variable with a subscript no greater than twenty. ALTAIR BASIC allows subscripts as high as DIM N$(255), check your version for the maximum subscript value. A variable can be dimensioned only once during each program in most BASICs, and it is assumed that any variable, whether subscripted or not, is equal to zero until the computer is told otherwise. It should be pointed out here also that some of the BASICs used in small computers require a DIM for all subscripted variables.

If you are dealing with a matrix or array that has columns and rows, a DIM statement should also be provided. DIM E(6,2) would define an array that has seven ROWs and three COLUMNS if your computer starts with zero rather than one.

MATH FUNCTIONS

The last major aspect of BASIC that will be discussed are the FUNCTIONS. BASICs differ considerably in the number of functions they support, but most have at least a few. A function is a lot like canned laughter on a TV program. Whenever the producer needs laughter, pushing the right button will produce it. Functions work the same way. If you need the square root of a number, for example, there is a function that will take care of it.

$$M = SQR(X)$$

In the example above, if X equals 9 then M will be assigned the value 3. The function SQR takes the square root of the variable in the parenthesis that follows. Other common functions are listed below with an explanation of how they operate:

SQR(A) — gives the square root of A. A must be a positive number, but can be a variable, a number, or an expression such as SQR(X/2*3.5).

INT(A) — finds the integer or whole number part of a number. If the number is positive it chops off everything to the right of the decimal. INT (12.3) equals 12 and INT (12.9) also equals 12. But negative numbers are rounded "up" to the next largest negative integer. Thus INT (-7.1) and INT(-7.7) both equal -8.

SIN(X) — You may not need these in the be-
COS(X)   ginning but they give the trig func-
TAN(X)   tions of a number — sine, cosine,
ATN(X)   tangent, and an arctangent.

ABS(X) — gives the absolute value of X. That
is, whether X is positive or negative, ABS(X) is always positive.
Note: Although X is used as the
variable in most of these examples
you can use any variable label you
wish: X has no special significance.

SGN(X) — gives a 1 if X is greater than 0, a
zero if it is equal to zero, and a -1
if it is less than zero.

RND(X) — in some BASICs this function will
give you a random number be-
tween 0 and 1. In many BASICs
the value of X makes no difference, the function operates the
same regardless. In some, however, RND works differently for
different types of X. If X is positive a different number will be
generated each time a random
number is called for in a program.
If X is 0 the same random number
is given over and over. And if X is
negative the same number will be
given later in a program if the
same X is used, but a different
negative number produces a different random number.

These are some of the most common math functions. Check
your manual to determine how many you can use. Most of them
are relatively easy to understand. The RND function does, how-

ever, need further comment since it is used so often in many
game programs. Here are three examples of the use of the RND
function:

```
10  PRINT RND(1)
20  PRINT RND(1)*10
30  LET X = RND(1)*10
40  PRINT INT(X)
```

Run this program and the computer should display a run that
produces a decimal number between 0 and 1 (line 10), which is
not that useful unless it is multiplied by 10 (line 20). That should
produce a more interesting number between 1 and 10. Lines 30
and 40 get rid of the fractional portion of the number and provide a crisp whole number between 0 and 9. Why just to nine?
Remember that with INT the decimal segment of the number is
"chopped off," not rounded up, even if the decimal is very close
to the next highest number. The value 9.9999999 still becomes 9
when the INT function is used. What if a number between 1 and
10 is needed? Lines 30 and 40 can be combined and a new component added to produce the desired results:

```
50 PRINT INT(10*RND(1)) + 1
```

In line 50 the computer begins with the innermost parentheses
and generates a random number between 0 and 1. It then multi-
plies it by 10 and applies the integer function to produce a whole
number. Finally the result is increased in value by one. The
result is a whole number between 1 and 10. In line 270 of the
Blackjack program, the random number was multiplied by 13
instead of 10 because there are 12 different cards to be "dealt."
Variations on these random number routines are found in hundreds of games that require a card to be dealt or dice to be
thrown.

STRING FUNCTIONS

In addition to the functions described above that deal with
numerical values there are a few which are designed specifically
for string variables:

LEN (A$) – indicates how long the string A$ is including letters, spaces, and punctuation.

LEFT$ (A$,X) – Suppose the string A$ is the word
RIGHT$(A$,X) BUSTED. PRINT LEFT$(A$,2) will cause the two leftmost letters (BU) to be printed. The RIGHT$ function works the same way. The first part tells the computer where to start (on the right or left), the string of interest is specified in the parentheses, and the number after the comma indicates how many letters are to be used in the operation B$ = LEFT(A$,3) would have B$ = LET if A$ = LETTER.

MID$(A$,X,Z) – MID$ works like the two functions above but the first number in the parentheses identifies the point in the string where the computer will begin and the second number tells how many letters are to be used. PRINT MID$(A$,2,3) produces UST if A$ is BUSTED – begin with the second letter and print three letters.

STR$(X) – STR$(X) changes the numerical
VAL(X$) value of X to a string. VAL(X$) does the reverse, a string becomes a numerical value. These are handy when you want to use a function applicable only to strings on a numerical value or vice versa. Note, however, that if a number (e.g., 99) is converted to a string it cannot be used in calculations unless it is reconverted to a numerical value.

TAB(X) — TAB(6) tells the computer to move over to the sixth print position from the left margin. If the program then says TAB(24) it will move over to the 24th position. Tab movement is always calculated from the left margin, it is not added to the value of the last TAB, nor is the position of the cursor considered. If the cursor is at position 24 and a TAB(23) occurs, an error message will be given. The function can be used only to move to the right.

This concludes the introduction to BASIC. The next chapter introduces you to the art and science of converting programs written in one version of BASIC to another.

CHAPTER 8

Converting from One BASIC to Another

Although large corporations may spend thousands of dollars on programs that will be used in their business, the small computer owner does not often have large sums of money to spend on software. Fortunately, however, he or she can take advantage of an increasing number of programs written in BASIC that are available at little or no cost in magazines, books, and through program exchanges. Games, business programs, and specialized programs regularly appear in most of the computer magazines. In fact, if you need a particular type of program you can buy a small booklet at many computer stores that contains a list of all the programs that have been published in computing magazines. By looking in the index it is possible to determine, for example, if a BASIC program on some business problem is available or if a particular game has been the subject of a programmer's efforts.

When a program interests you, check to see what version of BASIC was used when it was written. With luck it will be in a version that is supported on your computer. If not, it is often possible to modify the program so that it will run. Some suggestions and guidelines for making the conversion are provided in this chapter.

STEP 1. IS IT POSSIBLE?

Before trying to convert from one version to another, you should be very familiar with the BASIC used in your computer and with the general characteristics of the language. Do not try to modify a complicated program written in some exotic form of Extended BASIC so that it will run in a version of Tiny BASIC. The small versions have sacrificed so much that it is simply not possible to convert many programs. And in some cases a program will require so many modifications that the result is not worth the effort required. The time to discover that is before you start.

Once a particular program has been selected for modification, begin by looking carefully at all the commands and statements it uses. Before you actually start work, list all the incompatible commands and map out a general strategy for converting them. If some of the commands and statements used in the program are unfamiliar to you look them up in the next chapter. Once you understand what they do, be sure your version of BASIC has some means of doing the same thing before proceeding.

Tiny BASIC, for example, has no DIM statement and accepts no arrays or matrices at all while the Processor Technology 5K BASIC supports only single dimension arrays (e.g., DIM A (15)) and ALTAR 8K will accept an array with more than one dimension (e.g., DIM A (15,3,6)). These incompatibilities can be overcome but not without considerable effort. Some differences are, however, no more than cosmetic. PT 5K BASIC uses GET or XEQ as an instruction to begin reading information that has been stored on tape while Microsoft versions of BASIC use CLOAD. Most 8K BASICs will have a number of specialized functions and statements that allow you to do something with one instruction that would take several in the smaller versions. The same is true of the Extended BASICs. The ALTAIR 12K BASIC has all the features of their 8K and many enhancements as well.

STEP 2. MAKE CLERICAL CHANGES

BASICs differ considerably in the way routine matters are handled. Some, for example, allow the programmer to put more than one statement on a line. Others look for one, and only one, statement per line. It may thus be necessary to take a program that has multiple statements on some lines and to retype it with one statement or instruction per line.

Of those versions that do support multiple statements per line, there is some variation in the symbol that is used to tell the computer that what follows is a new and different statement. The first line below will run in some BASICs but not in TRS-80 BASIC. The second will run.

10 LET A = 6 + 4/PRINT A

10 LET A/6 + 4: PRINT A

Below are some clerical modifications that may be necessary. These examples should be considered as general models of the type of statements you are likely to encounter. Different variable names and numerical values will, of course, appear in a real program. To use this section you should identify all the statements in the program to be converted that are not accepted by your computer. Then check the examples below to determine if there is a simple solution to the incompatibility. In general, the modifications are stated as if the program were written in one of the rarer versions and you want to change it so that it will run in a more common version. If you have some rare BASIC, however, the modification may be in the other direction. In any case you will probably need to consult the next chapter which contains an alphabetical listing of most BASIC instructions along with conversion suggestions for many.

Rare Form		More Common Forms
RND (-X)	to	RND (X) or RND (0)
FRND (0)	to	RND (0)

The exact way RND statements are used varies considerably from version to version. Before making a change, be sure you know what the program expects the random function to accomplish and make sure that your change will do that.

A$ & B$ to A$ + B$

A$ and B$ are strings. Perhaps A$ is HELLO and B$ is the name of the person at the keyboard. The line above allows you to combine these two strings. A few versions use the "&" symbol to combine strings while most use the plus sign (+) for combining strings, just as you would do if you were combining two numbers instead of two strings.

SPC(X) to POS or POS(X) or TAB(X)

These functions allow the operator to position the cursor on the line in much the same way the space bar or tab key does on a typewriter. Again the way they work varies from BASIC to BASIC.

CLK$
DAT$
TIM$

There is usually no replacement for these if they are not a part of the version you use. PRINT CLK$ will cause the time, in hours, minutes, and seconds to be printed.

SST(X$,Y,Z) to MID(X$,Y,Z)

or MID$(X$,Y,Z) or STR(X$,Y,Z)

These are used to select a portion of a string with X$ specifying the string while Y and Z define where in the string selection begins and how much of the string is wanted.

IF...GOTO to IF...THEN

These are interchangeable statements. Smaller versions often support only the IF...THEN which is no problem since you need only change GOTO to THEN.

A$(5) to A$5
A(3) to A3

A string that belongs to a set of strings that are in an array is usually named using one of the formats in the first line. The names of numerical values in arrays use one of the formats on the second line.

QRT(9) to SQR(9)
LPRINT to PRINT

Different strokes for different folks. LPRINT may mean "print this on the printer not the CRT." If you don't have a printer it may be necessary to send everything to the screen using PRINT. QRT and SQR are two ways to say the same thing.

A$ to A

If your BASIC does not have special string functions it may be necessary to remove the $ from the variable labels. Lack of string handling functions will, however, usually mean that only the simpler programs can be converted.

** to Λ or ↑

The symbol used for powers is usually an "up arrow" of some sort, but a programmer will occasionally run into something else such as two stars. PRINT 5↑2 means "Print 5 squared" or 25.

PRINT 'HELLO' to PRINT "HELLO"

Quotation marks are almost universally used to enclose material that is to be printed as it stands. A few BASICs may use apostrophes instead.

10000 INPUT A to 99 INPUT A

Some small BASICs do not accept large line numbers. Determine the maximum number accepted by your system and re-number the program so that only valid line numbers are used. This is usually not a problem since there is nothing sacred about the number of a particular line. The numbers are simply used to tell the computer which line to read first (lowest number) and which to read next (next lowest number). Programmers generally avoid writing programs with consecutive line numbers (e.g., 1,2,3,4,5...) because a mistake that requires the addition of a new line somewhere in the program could mean every line must be renumbered and retyped. A desirable practice is to use line numbers that are multiples of five or even ten. That leaves plenty of room for modifications and additions. If large line numbers are a problem, however, it is perfectly acceptable to renumber the program so that the lines are incremented in multiples of two or three. In a pinch you can even number lines consecutively.

There are only two cautions that should be observed when renumbering lines. First, if at all possible leave some room for adding new lines later to deal with program errors or enhancements. Second, be sure to change statements that direct the program to a particular line (e.g., IF A = 5 GOTO 500) to reflect the new numbering scheme.

STEP 3. CONTENT CHANGES

The clerical changes discussed thus far generally require little
more than retyping an instruction in a slightly different format.
This type of conversion becomes almost second nature with
practice and presents few major problems. That is not true of
modifications to the actual content of the program. It is more
difficult to create the effects of an alien command, often from a
more powerful BASIC, in your own version. This is usually a
task for the experienced, although there are some common and
frequently encounted problems that can be dealt with by the
beginner.

In the chapter that follows most of the statements, commands
and punctuation marks found in BASIC are listed alphabetically along with a definition of their purpose and an example of
their effect in a typical instruction. Many of the entries end with
specific directions for converting the instruction using more
commonly available BASIC statements.

The following chapter is relatively comprehensive. It explains
well over 98% of the special words and symbols you will find in
BASIC programs, regardless of the version of BASIC used in
writing the program. Some things have, however, been omitted.
Commands unique to disk-based BASICs have not been included because they are often difficult to translate and because
little of the currently available inexpensive software requires
disk BASIC. Another type of BASIC statement that has been
omitted has to do with files. A file is an organized set of data
that is used in a program. If a researcher, for example, tests
each of the participants in an experiment he or she might put
the test scores of participants in a file. Then data in that
file might be used in several BASIC programs that compute
various statistical measures on the data in the file.

In actual fact the file may be a section of RAM, a portion of
cassette tape, or a location on a disk. In any case the file has a
name, and can be reached or located when necessary by name.
There is such diversity in the way files are handled from system-
to system that most of the statements and commands related to
their use will not be considered in detail. Some programs do use
file handling routines but the majority do not.

Aside from the two exceptions noted above, however, at least
some mention is made of virtually everything you're likely to encounter in any BASIC program.

CHAPTER 9

A Basic Glossary and Conversion Guide

A.

An abbreviation of ABS function.

ABS

A function that gives the absolute value of a number. If $X = -5$, ABS(X) will equal 5. ABS ignores the sign and makes everything positive.

Conversion — If you need ABS(X) try a substitution like this:

$$10 \text{ IF } X < 0 \text{ THEN } X = -X$$

AND

A Boolean logic function that will produce a -1 or a 0.

$$10 \text{ PRINT } X = 6 \text{ AND } Y = 7$$

If X does equal 6 and Y equals 7 then line 10 will produce a -1; if one or both of the conditions are untrue a 0 is printed.

Conversion — Here is a conversion model for BASICs that do not have the AND function:

```
10   IF X = 6 GOTO 30
20   PRINT 0: GOTO 60
30   IF Y = 7 GOTO 50
40   PRINT 0: GOTO 60
50   PRINT -1
60   ——— next line of program
```

Arrays and Subscripts

See Chapter 7. This section is an exception to the general rule that the chapter is organized alphabetically by the name of the BASIC statement, function, or command in question. It is hard to do that with arrays since they do not always require a word like DIM to be used. It may be the way things are arranged that makes the difference.

If you have one of the more powerful BASIC's it is likely that you can handle any of the milti-dimensioned arrays that might come along.

Smaller BASIC's, however, may be able to deal with two or three dimensions even if you don't have built-in features to handle them. Suppose a program has a dimensional array named T. T would have R rows and C columns.

$$20 \text{ DIM } T(R,C)$$

Now if $R = 4$ and $C = 3$ and if 1 is the lowest subscript value allowed, T will have four rows and three columns, a total of 12 separate values. If 0 is the lowest subscript, the array will have 15 separate values. Can we rewrite the program to avoid using a two dimensional array?

One solution is to relabel all the values in the array so that they become $T(1)$ (or T1), $T(2)...T(15)$ instead of $T(1,1)$, $T(1,2)$, $T(1,3)...T(4,3)$. The remainder of the program will also have to be rewritten to reflect the change. Values can be assigned to $T(1)$ through $T(15)$ by using READ DATA and a FOR NEXT loop:

```
10   FOR I = 0 TO 15
20   READ T(I)
30   NEXT I
40   DATA 4,6,12,3,4
```

Another solution is to "imitate" the double subscripted variable. Where $A(I,J)$ is the desired variable, the expression $A(C*(I-1) + J)$ can be substituted effectively. C is the number of columns in the array. Here are two equivalent programs resulting in the same printout, one of which uses the double subscript and the other of which does not:

Double Subscript	No Double Subscript
20 FOR I = 1 TO 3	10 DIM A(15)
30 FOR J = 1 TO 5	20 FOR I = 1 TO 3
40 A(I,J) = I + J/10	30 FOR J = 1 TO 5
50 PRINT A(I,J);	35 N = 5*(I-1) + J
60 NEXT J	40 A(N) = I + J/10
70 PRINT	50 PRINT A(N);
80 NEXT I	60 NEXT J
	70 PRINT
	80 NEXT I

RUN

```
1.1   1.2   1.3   1.4   1.5
2.1   2.2   2.3   2.4   2.5
3.1   3.2   3.3   3.4   3.4
```

ASC

Converts a string or character into a number. For example, the ASCII binary code for A is 01000001 which is 65 decimal or 41 hex.

```
10  IF A$ = A THEN PRINT ASC(A$)
RUN
65
```

Conversion—ASC is hard to convert if it is not available. When absolutely necessary, it might be possible to use a series of IF THEN statements arranged in a table (e.g., IF A$ = A THEN PRINT 65, IF A$ = B THEN...).

Some BASIC's treat ASC a little differently. They may allow you to use ASC on a long string (e.g., A$ = ARKANSAS), but use only the first letter for ASC(A$). In this case use LEFT$ or the equivalent when converting. Other BASIC's do this:

$$ASC(A\$(X))$$

with X standing for the number of the character to be used. If

A$ = ARKANSAS then ASC(A$,3) would take K as the letter to work with.

AT

A function in TRS-80 Level 1 BASIC that tells the computer where to start printing:

10 PRINT AT 540,"THIS IS"

Radio Shack's video display is divided into 16 lines of 64 characters. Position 540 is in about the middle of the video screen and that is where "THIS IS" would be printed.

Conversion—If changing to Level II TRS-80 BASIC, just replace AT with @. For other BASICs you may be able to use TAB or PRINT with an appropriate number of spaces enclosed in quotation marks to accomplish the same thing. POKE is also a possibility. POKE the proper code into the correct memory location (the one that is used to store the display character code for that screen location.)

ATAN or ATN

Both compute the arctangent of the number that follows the statement, (e.g., ATN(3)) in radians. See LOG Functions for more details.

BASE

Defines the base variable in an array. Most BASICs assume an array starts with 1. Thus DIM A(3) means there is an A(1), A(2), and A(3). If you put BASE(0) before the DIM A(3) statement, however, it will produce an array of A(0), A(1), A(2), and A(3); one more than before. Most computers allow you to use BASE only once, if at all, in each program. Most allow only 0 or 1 as an argument, so that the first element in an array is 0 or 1. A few BASICs allow higher numbers, e.g., BASE 4. In this case the first element in an array would be given the argument 4 (e.g., A(4)).

Conversion—Working around BASE may be difficult, or at least complex. Where all arrays must begin with element 1 change the sections of the program that make use of the array so

that the correct element is used (e.g., change PRINT A(0) to
PRINT A(1)).

```
10  BASE 0
20  DIM A(5)        original program
25  A(0) = 265
30  PRINT A(0)

10  DIM A(6)        converted program to avoid
25  A(1) = 265      using BASE
30  PRINT A(1)
```

BREAK

In TI BASIC the statement BREAK causes the computer to
halt when the line specified is encountered.

10 BREAK 360

Line 10 tells the computer to stop executing instructions when it
reaches line 360. Your computer may have an equivalent statement, or it may be possible to rewrite the program so that the
same purpose is accomplished in a different way.

C.

Same as CONTINUE or CONT on some computers (e.g.,
TRS-80 Level I). Tells the computer to continue executing the
program after a halt.

CALL

This function is similar to USR. Both create a link between a
machine language program and a BASIC program.

10 CALL 16234

Line 10 tells the computer to go to memory location 16234
(decimal) and execute the program found there. The exact way
CALL works varies from BASIC to BASIC. The number desig-
nating the memory location where the machine language program is stored may be decimal, as above, or hexadecimal. Some

BASICs even allow you to create a machine language routine, give it a name, and then access it by name (e.g., CALL JOE). Adjust any CALLS you find to fit your BASIC. Two more points that have to be considered in converting CALL statements are the machine language program itself and the spot in memory where it is placed.

A machine language program is usually not portable — it is unlikely that it can be placed intact in another computer and work. I/O ports, for example, are numbered differently to name but one of the potential problems. In addition, computers vary considerably as to the location of suitable RAM for storing machine language routines. It's a conversion effort that might be too difficult for many beginners.

CALL CHAR(#,#)

Used in TI BASIC to redefine the ASCII character specified by the first number so that it now stands for the graphic pattern specified by the second number.

CDBL

Makes a single precision number a double precision number. That is, the accuracy of the number is extended from 6 digits to 17 digits. Consider the program below:

```
10   X = 5: Y = 6
20   PRINT X/Y
30   PRINT CDBL(X/Y)
```

When run it produces the following output:

```
RUN
.833333
.833333134651184
```

The second line is more accurate as a result of the CDBL function.

Conversion — In many programs you may be able to obtain satisfactory (but less accurate) results simply by removing CDBL. In the sample program above you would use line 20 instead of line 30. Another function, DEFDBl, may be a useful substitute if the program can be modified to suit DEFDBL. See also # at the end of the glossary.

CHANGE

Similar to CHR$, ASC, and VAL, this function takes each letter or symbol in a string and converts them to their ASCII numeric code.

```
10  A$ = CHANGE
20  CHANGE A$ TO N
```

The two lines above define a string, A$, and then change each character to a numeric value which is stored in an array named N. N(0) will equal the ASCII code for C (which is 43 hex) N(1) will equal 48 hex (the code for H) and so on. CHANGE can also be used in the reverse.

```
10  N(0) = 67
20  N(1) = 65
30  N(2) = 82
40  CHANGE N TO A$
```

Now A$ will equal CAR if the BASIC in use assumes the numbers 67, 65, and 82 are decimal ASCII codes (67 = C, 65 = A, 82 = R).

Conversion — Use CHR$, ASC or VAL to convert each element individually (e.g., N(0)...).

CHAR, CHAR#, CHR

These three functions are very similar. PRINT CHAR(#,#) will print a character specified by the first number in the parentheses following CHAR. The number is the ASCII decimal code for the character you want. For A it is 65, B is 66 and so forth. The second number specifies the number of letters to be placed in the string. Default is 5.

CHAR$ and CHR operate the same as CHAR except only one number is placed in the parentheses — the decimal number of the ASCII character desired. For "C" you would use PRINT CHAR$(67) or PRINT CHR(67).

Conversion—Try substituting among the three forms of this function. Change CHAR(120) to CHAR$(120) or CHR(120). If none of the three work in a program that uses the function extensively try rewriting the program to use a function like ASC or CHR$.

CHR$

Same as CHR, CHAR$ in that it will produce an ASCII symbol if its decimal code is provided—CHR$(#). Some BASICs also use this function to print graphic symbols or to perform a special control function (e.g., clear the screen).

Conversion—If CHR$ is simply providing an ASCII symbol such as a letter or number, try replacing it with CHAR$, CHR$, or CHAR. If it is being used to produce a particular action such as turning on a tape recorder, you have a more serious problem. Another function or statement may be available to accomplish the same purpose. If graphics are involved you must translate the graphics of the original computer into those used by your machine, if you have any. Good luck. HINT: POKE might work in some conversion efforts.

CINT

Converts a number to its integer value. This is a very useful rounding function that will produce whole numbers from a number with a decimal portion.

```
10   X = 6.8
20   Y = -6.8
30   PRINT CINT(X)
40   PRINT CINT(Y)
RUN
 6
-7
```

Positive numbers are rounded down (the decimal portion is chopped off) while negative numbers are rounded to the next most negative number.

Conversion—Sometimes INT will serve the same purpose although INT may permanently change the number into an integer. It is also possible to use IF THEN when there is a limited range of numbers to be changed. Suppose X can be any value between 0 and 6.999999:

```
10  IF X<1 THEN X = 0
20  IF X>1 THEN X = 1
30  IF X>2 THEN X = 2
40  IF X>3 THEN X = 3
50  IF X>4 THEN X = 4
60  IF X>5 THEN X = 5
70  IF X>6 THEN X = 6
```

CLEAR

Resets all variables to 0 and erases all strings.

```
10  A = 10
20  A$ = "HERE TODAY"
30  B = 20
35  PRINT "BEFORE CLEAR"
40  PRINT A,A$,B
50  CLEAR
55  PRINT "NOW AFTER
CLEAR"
60  PRINT A,B$,B
RUN
BEFORE CLEAR
10          HERE TODAY          20
NOW AFTER CLEAR
0                                0
```

Conversion — If your computer doesn't have CLEAR you can reset all variables in the program individually (e.g., X = 0, A$ = "",B = 0). A few BASICs add a number after CLEAR which defines the number of bytes set aside for strings. If this must be done in a different way look for the method used in your BASIC and use it. Do you know the default for string space in your BASIC, that is, the number of bytes set aside to store strings? One final note. Typing RUN in most BASICs also results in a CLEAR being performed.

CLK$ CLK

These functions provide the time in hours, minutes, and seconds. There is no substitute for these (unless TIM or TIME is available) but you may be able to work around them by rewriting the program.

CLOG(#)

This function computes the common log of any number greater than 0. The number is placed in the parentheses. See Log Functions.

CLR

Sometimes used as an abbreviation for CLEAR. Just replace CLR with CLEAR. See CLEAR for conversion possibilities.

CLS

Used to "clear screen". Many computers have a CLEAR key that does the same thing. Push it and all the material on the screen is erased.

Conversion — If you have a CLEAR key but no CLEAR command it means the key outputs a code that clears the screen. If you can cause the program to print that code, it is often possible to obtain a CLEAR. For many computers the code is a 24. Thus PRINT CHR$(24) may be the same as CLEAR. If 24 doesn't work try other numbers. If the search for a number isn't successful you can always use a series of PRINTS to clear the screen.

```
10   FOR X = 1 TO 16
20   PRINT " "
30   X = X + 1
40   NEXT X
```

This routine will clear a 16 line screen but the cursor may still be at the bottom of the screen instead of at the top.

COLOR

A command in Apple II BASIC that is used to display one of 16 colors at a specified screen location. It would be very difficult to convert a program using this command.

"CONTROL" – –

Pushing the control key and another key at the same time causes the computer to do all sorts of things. Some common combinations are given below:

CTRL C stops program execution, helps you regain control of a computer that runs amuck.

CTRL G rings the bell on a Teletype and many other printers.

COPY

Used by some BASICs to cause a printer to begin operating. You may have to use something like LPRINT to change the output port from the CRT to a printer. In some systems each port has a number which is used in a SET command. SET 0 = 1 on a SOL will cause further output to go to the serial output port. If a printer is attached, the output will appear on it.

COS(#)

Calculates COSINE of the angle specified by the number in parentheses. The answer is given in radians rather than degrees (1 radian = 57.29578 degrees, 1 degree = .0174533 radians). See Log Functions.

CSNG

Changes a previously defined double precision number to a single precision number. See CDBL or DBL for more information. In essence the number is "rounded off" to six significant digits.

```
10   A = 15.463278142601
20   PRINT CSGN(X)
RUN
15.4633
```

Conversions – DEFSNG may be a usable substitute for CSNG although some program modifications may be required.

CURSOR #1,#2

A PT Extended BASIC statement that places the cursor at a specified location on the screen. PT's SOL has a 16 line by 64 character display.

10 CURSOR 6,50

Line 10 places the cursor on line 6, position 50. The next character to be printed will appear at that location.

Conversion — PRINT @ or its equivalent may be a suitable substitute, but you will have to determine just where on the screen the material is to be printed and adjust the program accordingly.

D

Used to define a number as double precision when the number is expressed in scientific notation.

$1.26054D + 10$ — a double precision number which will have 16 significant digits.

$1.26054E + 10$ — a single precision number which has 8 significant digits. See E also.

DAT

Abbreviation for DATA.

DATA

See Chapter 6. There are some variations in use. You may or may not be able to put strings (A, AB) in DATA statements. If strings are O.K., it may not be necessary to enclose them in quotations (e.g., "A", "AB", "ABC"). If strings are not acceptable it is not difficult to convert most programs to the use of IN-PUT and LET statements in place of READ DATA.

DEFFN

This is a very practical function that is used to create additional functions. In a program that performs a particular computation over and over it may save time and memory to use DEF to create a special function that does the computation you need. Suppose a program requires that the variable X be squared, then divided by 5. We could call that Function "A" or "FNA" and use DEF to create it:

$$DEF\ FNA(X) = (X*X/5).$$

(The letter in the parentheses after FNA is a "dummy variable"). It must match the letter on the other side of the equal sign. A simple example of its use is shown below:

```
10  X = 10
20  DEF FNA(X) = X*X/5)
30  PRINT FNA(X)
RUN
20
```

The example above illustrates the simplest user defined function. Extended BASICs can get very fancy with functions that have more than one variable, or take more than one line. Suppose a program frequently calls for X squared to be added to Y squared. It can be done this way:

```
10  X = 5: Y = 4
20  DEF FNA(X,Y) = (X*X) + (Y*Y)
30  PRINT FNA
RUN
41
```

Thus far only numeric variables have been used. Some BASICs also permit string variables but the proper designation must be used (e.g., DEF FNA$).

A user defined function also need not fit on a single line. Many extended BASICs accept multiple line functions. Here is an example:

```
10  DEF FNA1(L,S)
20  X = 0
30  FOR I = 1 TO L
40  X = X + L*S
50  NEXT I
60  RETURN X
70  FNEND
```

This is a complex, multiple line, user-defined function. The two variables that are used in it are placed in the parentheses on line 10. A1 specifies the name attached to the results of the first pass through the loop that defines the function. The second pass will define A2, and so on with the number of passes determined by L. FNEND is placed at the end of the user defined function to tell the computer where the routine ends.

Conversions — A good understanding of defined functions is necessary in order to successfully convert. If you have DEF but it isn't working as written, check for minor incompatibilities such as a program that defines the same user function more than once. If your computer won't accept that, you may be able to rename one of the functions and make it work. In other cases the incompatibility will be in the complexity of the function. Multiple line functions can be broken into several single line functions that use the results of a preceding function in computing another.

And if you have no DEF at all in your BASIC remember it is only a convenience; it can be rewritten using standard functions. In the first example, line 30 could be written as:

$$30 \quad \text{PRINT (X*X)/5}$$

A last resort, then, is to simply write out each function rather than using the shorthand of the DEF function.

DEFDBL

Declares a particular variable as double precision.

>   20   DEFDBL X
>   30   X = A/B
>   40   PRINT X

If A = 36 and B = 25 then X would equal 1.44000 as a single precision number. As a double number it would be 1.440000057220459.

Conversion — One DEFDBL is often used to make several variables double precision. If you can't use one DEFDBL to make several variables double precision, break the function up into single variable functions where needed. For example, if DEFDBL A — C doesn't work try DEFDBL A: DEFDBL B: DEFDBL C. See also CDBL and DBL.

DEFINT

Declares the variables that are listed after it are integers or whole numbers (e.g., DEFINT A, B, C). Numbers with decimal components are rounded to their whole components.

```
10  DEFINT A
20  A = 6.22
30  PRINT A
RUN
6
```

Conversion — Some BASICs may allow only one variable in a DEFINT statement. If so change:

```
10  DEFINT A,B
          to
10  DEFINT A
15  DEFINT B
```

If you don't have the function it is usually possible to replace it with INT.

DEFSNG

Defines a variable as single precision. Works just like DEFD-BL. See DEFDBL, CSN, CBBL for ideas on conversion.

DEFSTR

Defines the variable that follows as a string variable. It works just like adding a $ to a variable.

DEFSTR A, B, C

is the same as adding a $ after each letter (A$, B$, C$).

Conversion — As might be expected, the $ can be used in place of DEFSTR. It is a little more trouble to put all those $ signs in, but it does help you keep string and numeric variables straight. Some BASICs may also require a DIM to specify the number of bytes of memory that should be set aside for each string. DIM first, then create the string.

DEG

When this appears in a program the trig functions that are computed afterward are done in degrees rather than radians. RAD changes it back to figuring in radians.

Conversion—Use radians times 57.29578 and you obtain an answer that is in degrees thus eliminating the need for DEG.

If DEG has a number in parentheses after it the function will convert the radian number in the parentheses to degrees.

10   PRINT DEG(26)

The same thing can be done by multiplying radians times 57.29578.

10   PRINT 26*57.29578

DIM

See chapter 7.

Conversion—DIM works differently in the various BASICs. A few small interpreters won't accept more than a certain number of variables and thus won't allow many DIM statements. TRS-80 Level I, for example, allows only two arrays, A and B. If you have more than two arrays it is thus necessary to rewrite the program so that the elements of the third array (e.g., C(0), C(1), C(2), C(3)...) are treated as separate entities rather than as parts of an array. Level I BASIC, in fact, doesn't require DIM to be used at all. It will use all the available memory, if necessary, to store data for an array. Other BASICs are not so altruistic. They want to know exactly how much memory to set aside. DIM A(6) will set aside space for 7 elements (0-6) which will have the names A(0), A(1), A(2), A(3), A(4), A(5), and A(6). One potential problem is incompatibility between BASICs that assume A(1) is the lowest element and those that assume there is an A(0) as the first element. A(0) is to be the standard in future BASICs.

Most small BASIC interpreters have a default value for arrays. In many it is assumed a list will have no more than 11 elements while an array will be no more than a two dimensional 11 by 11 array. So long as you have no more than that, there is no need for a DIM. Since the default value varies, however, it may sometimes be necessary to add a DIM to keep your BASIC happy.

It is generally permissible to use DIM to specify the length of a string as well. DIM N$(20), for example, could be used to set aside space for the string N$ which could contain as many as 20 characters. Some BASICs do not have strings defined by $ and thus won't accept string dimensioning; dropping the $ sometimes eliminates the problem. Others require every string to be dimensioned; there is no default value.

A final potential problem is the use of double or triple dimensions. See Chapter 7 for help on this. See also Arrays in this chapter.

E

Indicates scientific or exponential notation. 4.50E + 6 is the same as 4500000. The number 4.50E + 6 is a single precision number that can be written in a more familiar way by moving the decimal point 6 places to the right. If it were 4.50E − 6 the decimal point would move to the left (.0000045). It's an easy way to write big numbers or very precise decimal fractions.

E

Abbreviation for END.

ELSE

Used to develop a more sophisticated IF THEN statement.

```
10  IF X = 0 THEN 50 ELSE 60
20  ─── next line of program
```

Line 10 tells the computer to branch to line 50 if X = 0. It also tells the computer to go to 60 if X does not equal 0. If we drop ELSE 60 from line 10 the computer will drop to line 20 if X<>0. If, however, we add line 15 it will serve the same purpose as ELSE 60.

```
10  IF X = 0 THEN 50
15  IF X<>0 THEN 60
20  ───
```

END

The more ancient versions of BASIC required the word END

on the last line of the program. Most of the BASICs for small computers can take it or leave it. END makes no difference in how the program runs. A few don't recognize END at all and will give you an error message if it isn't removed completely from the program. If that happens to you just delete END. See STOP also.

EQ

Used instead of = sign in some BASICs.

EQV

A logic function. If A and B are both 0 or both 1 when line 10 below is executed a 1 will be printed; if A equals 1 and B equals 0, or vice versa, a 0 will be printed.

10   PRINT A EQV B

EXAM

Operates the same as PEEK. See PEEK for details. If you don't have EXAM use PEEK.

EXIT

Causes the computer to leave an active FOR NEXT loop and begin executing programs at line #. Conversion involves finding another way to get execution to branch to the proper line. Some BASICs will not allow you to exit a FOR NEXT loop before it is completed; check your BASIC manual for alternatives.

EXP(#)

This function computes the natural log of the number that is in parentheses. See Log Functions.

F.

Abbreviation for FOR.

FETCH(#)

Works just like PEEK. See PEEK. PRINT FETCH (1000) will print the value stored in memory location 1000.

FILL #,#

Works same as POKE. FILL 1000,32 puts the value 32 in memory location 1000. FILL will put any value between 0 and 255 (the largest decimal value that can be expressed in one 8 bit byte) into the memory location specified by the first number after FILL. See POKE.

FIX(#)

Removes the fractional part of a number.

```
10   A = 12.431
20   PRINT FIX(A)
RUN
12
```

FIX is very similar to INT, except negative numbers are not rounded down—that is a -12.6 does not become -13 if FIX is used. It does, however, with INT. In many instances this is not a crucial difference and INT can be used in place of FIX.

FN

See DEF

FNEND

See DEF

G.

Abbreviation for GOTO

GE

Used instead of $\geq$ (greater than or equal to).

GO

See chapter 7. Most BASICs accept either GOTO or GO TO but a few will insist on one or the other only.

GOS.

Abbreviation for GOSUB.

GOSUB

See chapter 7.

GOTO

See chapter 7.

GOTO OF

This is a very sophisticated branching statement. Here is an example:

```
10   GOTO A OF 50,60,70
20  ———
```

Line 10 tells the computer that it should branch to line 50 if A = 1, to line 60 if A = 2, and line 70 if A = 3. If the integer value of A is not 1, 2, or 3 the computer will simply move on to line 20. Very similar to ON GOTO.

Conversion — use ON-GOTO or the method described for converting ELSE:

```
10   IF A = 1 GOTO 50
12   IF A = 2 GOTO 60
15   IF A = 3 GOTO 70
```

GR

In Apple BASIC GR changes the computer display from text to graphics. When GR is read several special graphics statements can be used to create sophisticted pictures, figures, and tables. Conversion would be very difficult.

GT

Used instead of > (greater than).

HEX$(#)

This function takes the integer decimal number in the parentheses and converts it to its hexadecimal equivalent.

```
10   A = 92
20   PRINT HEX$(A)
RUN
5B
```

Conversion—Several programs have appeared in the magazines that can be used to convert from one number base to another. Some of them are:

R. Broucke, Conversions between octal and hexadecimal. *Dr. Dobb's Journal,* June, 1977.

I. Doliner, CONVBASE: Getting down to bases. *Interface Age,* November, 1977.

P. Hughes, HEXDEC...hexadecimal to decimal conversion. *Kilobaud,* August, 1977.

J. Swain, Number base conversion routine. *Interface Age,* May, 1977.

J. West, Changing bases (BASIC), *Creative Computing,* November, 1977.

M. Winkler, Number base conversion program. *Interface Age,* November, 1977.

HLIN AT

An Apple BASIC graphics statement used to produce a horizontal line at a specific place on the screen.

HOME

Places the cursor in the top left hand corner of the screen. Your BASIC may use some other word to accomplish the same thing. See CLS also.

I.

Abbreviation for INT

IF

See chapter 7.

IF GOSUB

See chapter 7. If your computer has IF THEN but not IF GOSUB you can substitute IF THEN with some adjustments. Here is a model.

```
10  IF X = 0 GOSUB 500
20  ———— next line of program
         replace line 10 with
10  IF X = 0 GOTO 500
```

and at the end of the subroutine that starts at line 500 add another instruction GOTO 20. That will get you back to the main line of the program without using GOSUB.

IF GOTO

See chapter 7. You may find it necessary to use IF THEN GOTO or simply IF THEN.

IF THE

Abbreviation for IF THEN.

IF THEN

See Chapter 7. Most, if not all, BASICs have IF THEN, but the way it is used varies. Generally if the condition specified after IF is met the computer branches to the line specified after THEN.

10   IF A<0 THEN 120

In line 10 above a GOTO is understood, but need not be written. It may be necessary to insert GOTO after THEN or replace THEN with GOTO. The reverse of these suggestions may also be required (e.g., add THEN or replace GOTO with THEN).

IF THEN serves other purposes besides branching, at least in some BASICs. Here are some examples.

```
10   IF A<0 THEN LET B = A*B
20   IF A<0 THEN PRINT "THAT'S ALL"
30   IF A<0 THEN END
```

BASICs that do not support such IF THEN statements will require lines such as the three above to be broken down so that the decision is on one line, IF A<0 THEN 650, and the work to be done is on another, 650 LET B = A*B.

20   IF A – B<0 THEN 150

If you can't use a line like 20 then use the following as a model for modification:

```
20   LET C = A – B
30   IF C<0 THEN 150
```

IN.

Abbreviation for INPUT

INKEY$

A TRS-80 Level II function that "reads" a keypress. The most common use of this function is in a loop that cycles round and round until a key is pressed. Here is an example:

```
10   A$ = INKEY$
20   IF A = "" THEN 10
30   PRINT "WE GOT PAST THE INKEY$!"
```

As long as no key is pressed at the instant the INKEY$ function looks for a keypress, A will equal 0 and line 20 will cause the computer to loop back to 10. Line 20 compares A$ to a "null string" or a string with nothing in it. But as soon as INKEY$ detects that a key on the keyboard has been pressed it will move on to 30. INKEY$ is often used to pace the presentation of material on the screen. A full screen of instructions may appear on the screen. Then some routine like lines 10-30 above is used to stop the display until the user finishes reading the material. As soon as all the instructions on the screen have been read any key can be pressed and the program will move one to display more instructions or whatever.

Conversion—There will usually be some way around using INKEY$ if it is not available. Lines 10-30 could be rewritten, for example, using INPUT:

```
10   INPUT D
30   PRINT "WE GOT PAST IT AGAIN!"
```

D is an irrelevant or unused variable. Its only purpose is to stop the computer. As soon as a number is pressed it will proceed to line 30. You could use D$ instead of D and have the user press a letter such as G (for GO). The disadvantages of using INPUT is that RETURN or ENTER must be pressed as well.

INP(#)

Causes the computer to read the current value that appears at the port whose number is specified by #.

10   PRINT INP(1)

If you have a computer whose keyboard is input port 1, and if you were pressing 2 when line 10 is executed the "2" will appear on the screen. Conversion of INP depends on the method used in your system to specify an input port. INKEY$ would do the same thing on a TRS-80 if the keyboard is the input device. To convert, determine what the instruction is trying to do (e.g., which port will it look to) and use whatever methods are available in your system to accomplish it (e.g., monitor system commands).

INPUT

See Chapters 6 and 7. Simple INPUT statements can be handled by almost all BASICs. Several forms of INPUT may be a problem.

INPUT(#)A$

This special version of INPUT allows the programmer to specify exactly how many keypresses are to be accepted and assigned to A$.

10 INPUT(3)A$

Line 10 will expect the user to input 3 characters which will be assigned to A$. As soon as 3 characters have been entered it moves on to the next line; there is no need to press the carriage return or Enter key.

10 INPUT(1)A

This line 10 would expect one key, representing a number from 0 to 9 to be pressed, which would be assigned to A. It is even possible to set a time limit for responding. The time is in tenths of a second.

10 INPUT(1,50) "DO YOU WANT INSTRUCTIONS?",R$

Line 10 waits 5 seconds for one keypress, probably a "Y" or "N" and assigns it to R$.

Conversion—The fancier INPUT commands can usually be reduced to their simpler cousins without completely destroying the program.

INPUTL

Operates the same as INPUT except there is no automatic carriage return after the data is input. That is, the material that is printed next will appear on the same line as the data input. If you don't have INPUTL it will usually be possible to use IN-PUT instead. Try adding a comma or semicolon after the IN-PUT statement if it is absolutely necessary to have whatever is printed next on the same line.

INT

Rounds a number off to its whole number value. If $A = 6.2$, INT(A) will equal 6. The decimal part of the number is dropped, not rounded up or down, so that $A = 6.9$, INT(A) still equals 6. A negative number is rounded to the next most negative number. If $A = -6.2$ then INT(A) will equal 7.

LE

Used instead of $\leqslant$ (less than or equal to).

LEFT(string) and LEFT$(string)

This function takes the string specified in the parentheses and identifies a specific subset of the symbols that make up the string.

```
10   PRINT LEFT("DEMO",2)
RUN
DE
```

Line 10 above says "print the leftmost two characters of the string "DEMO." The two lines below do the same thing.

```
10  A$ = "DEMO"
20  PRINT LEFT (A$,2)
RUN
DE
```

If LEFT doesn't work try LEFT$. Some BASICs use the following form instead of LEFT:

```
10  PRINT (A$,1,2)
```

Line 10 says "starting from the first character on the left print the next two characters."

LEN

Calculates the number of characters in a string. If A$ = "DOLLY", PRINT LEN A$ will print a 5 since DOLLY has 5 letters. Converting LEN would be difficult.

LET

See Chapter 6. The only hassle you may encounter with LET has to do with the fact that some BASICs require the use of a LET when defining variables while others assume it.

```
10  LET A = 5        should work in all BASICs
10  A = 5            works in most but not all
```

LGT(#)

Calculates the common log of any number greater than 0. See Log Functions.

LIN(#)

This statement is used to make the computer skip a specified number of lines before printing the output that follows. It is a convenient means of spacing between material.

Conversion — 10 LIN(5) will put 5 blank lines between output. So will the following:

```
10  PRINT " "
20  PRINT " "
30  PRINT " "
40  PRINT " "
50  PRINT " "
    or
10  FOR B = 1 TO 5
12  PRINT " "
14  NEXT B
```

LN(#)

Computes the natural log of any number greater than 0. See Log Functions.

LOG FUNCTIONS

I have not included a complete set of conversion programs for the wide variety of logarithmic functions found in the various BASICs. One reason is that they are not used that often by many programmers, and those who do tend to need them very often. If you need log function conversion programs, see one of the sources listed below:

L. Dishman, Log Functions in BASIC. *Personal Computing,* January, 1979.

D. Allison, Quick and Dirty Functions for BASIC, *Dr. Dobb's Journal,* $29, p. 13-16.

D. Lein, *The BASIC Handbook.* San Diego: Compusoft Publishing Company, 1978.

LOG(#)   LOGE(#)   LOG10(#)

The three statements above compute the natural log of any number greater than 0. See Log Functions.

LONG

Used to define a variable as double precision. See DEFDBL for more information. DEFDBL may be a good substitute.

LT

Used instead of < (less than sign).

LPRINT

This statement is used in several BASICs to send output to the printer. PRINT "HERE IT IS" will appear on the screen while LPRINT "HERE IT IS" will appear on the printer.

Conversion—If you don't have a printer we don't have a BASIC statement that will create one for you. Changing all LPRINTs to to PRINTs will direct everything to the screen for display. If you do have a printer check to see how your BASIC and your operating system software send output to it. Some use SET commands, others have a BASIC command, and others use LPRINT.

MARGIN

Resets the maximum line length permitted.

10   MARGIN 90

Line 10 allows up to 90 characters to be printed on a line before an automatic carriage return is generated. Few BASICs allow this sort of thing in the middle of a program. The ones that have anything similar usually do it once before a program is run. It would probably be best to rewrite the program so that it uses the standard line length in your system.

MAT or MATRIX

MAT stands for MATRIX and is part of a whole series of advanced statements that can work on large sets of data. Each of the most frequently encountered MAT statements will be presented and explained. Conversion, if you can't use MAT, usually involves revising the MAT sections of the program using simpler statements. The program will be longer, but should work fine.

MAT CON and MAT ZER

Sets every element in an array to equal 1. MAT A = CON sets every element in A to equal 1. A will have been dimensioned by an earlier DIM statement. MAT ZER works the same way but sets all the elements to equal zero.

MAT INPUT

This is one of several statements that combine MAT with a more familiar word. MAT INPUT causes the computer to wait for data to be input which will be assigned to each of the elements in A. If A has been dimensioned to have 6 elements (e.g., DIM A(6)) the computer will allow you to input up to 6 values with all except the last one followed by a comma (e.g., 2,4,6,8,10,12). If you have to input so much data it won't fit on one line you can replace the last comma on a line with an ampersand (&) and press carriage return. Then continue to input data on the following line.

10 DIM A(5)	Tells the computer there will be 6 elements in A (A(0), A(1), A(2), A(3), A(4), A(5)).
20 MAT INPUT A	When the computer reads line 20 it will print a "?" and wait to receive input from the keyboard.

If you type "15", for example, and hit RETURN or ENTER element A(0) will now equal 15 and the computer will print a double "??" because it is looking for data to assign to A(1) through A(5). If instead, the following is typed in:

$$15,14,14,10,11,6$$

and RETURN pressed the computer will assign the six numbers separated by a comma to A(0) through A(5). See DIM for additional information.

Conversion — FOR NEXT loops can be used in place of MAT INPUT. Here is a conversion for the program given earlier.

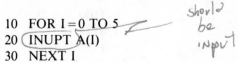

```
10   FOR I = 0 TO 5
20   INUPT A(I)
30   NEXT I
```
should be input

The only difference between the MAT INPUT and FOR NEXT

program is that the MAT INPUT allows the user to type in all the numbers at once, if they are separated by commas. FOR NEXT requires them to be INPUT one at a time with RETURN or ENTER pressed after each. Unfortunately, the example above is adequate only for the simplest MAT INPUT statement. Here is a more complicated example.

```
 5   DIM A(2,5)
10   MAT INPUT A
```

This program will accept data for a two dimensional array, "A" will have 18 elements as diagramed below:

$$A(0,0) \quad A(0,1) \quad A(0,2)$$
$$A(1,0) \quad A(1,1) \quad A(1,2)$$
$$A(2,0) \quad A(2,1) \quad A(2,2)$$
$$A(3,0) \quad A(3,1) \quad A(3,2)$$
$$A(4,0) \quad A(4,1) \quad A(4,2)$$
$$A(5,0) \quad A(5,1) \quad A(5,2)$$

The first number (2 in our example) specifies the rows in the array while the second (5) indicates the columns. NOTE: some systems reverse the order with columns listed first and rows next. The example also assumes the first element in the array will be A(0,0) rather than A(1,1). Again BASICs differ on this point. In some BASICs, even those that use 0 as the base element, MAT instructions begin with element 1 (e.g., A(1,1)) and ignore all elements with zero subscripts. See Arrays in this chapter. MAT INPUT A will ask for 18 different values for A(0,0) through A(5,2). Converting to FOR NEXT loops requires use of nested loops.

```
 5   DIM A(5,2)
10   FOR I = 0 TO 2
12   FOR L = 0 TO 5
14   INPUT A(I,L)
16   NEXT L
18   NEXT I
```

Be careful with the nested loops. If your computer does not allow two dimensional arrays you can still use a program with MAT INPUT by using many simple input statements. You may have to change the names of the variables:

$$A(0,0) = A0$$
$$A(0,1) = A1$$
$$A(0,2) = A2$$
$$A(1,0) = A3$$
$$A(1,1) = A4$$
$$A(1,2) = A5$$

Don't forget to change all the parts of the program that are affected.

MAT PRINT

Works a lot like MAT INPUT. MAT PRINT A will cause the computer to print out all the values of the elements of A. Generally the elements are spaced out with 5 on a line.

```
10   DIM A(5)
20   MAT PRINT A
```

Line 20 will print 6 values, those assigned to A(0) through A(5). Generally where these six values are printed can be determined by the use of a comma or semicolon after the variable name.

MAT PRINT A,	data is spaced across line as if TAB were used
MAT PRINT A;	data printed much closer together.

Like MAT INPUT, MAT PRINT will work with multidimensioned arrays. Conversion techniques are similar to MAT IN-PUT except PRINT is used in the FOR NEXT loops instead of INPUT.

MAT READ

Reads values from a DATA statement and assigns the values

to an array. The operation is very similar to MAT INPUT and
MAT PRINT. See the other MAT statements for more information. You may or may not have to use DIM statements (usually
not if there are less than 10 elements in the array). When converting use the examples in MAT INPUT and substitute READ
for INPUT in the FOR NEXT loops.

All the basic arithmetic operations (and some that are not so
basic) can be performed on matrices. Here are some typical
instructions:

MAT C = A + B   Means a new matrix, C, is created by
adding together the appropriate elements in A and B. For example, C(1,1) would equal A(1,1) plus B(1,1). Subtraction works
just like addition (e.g., MAT C = A − B). Matrices A and B
must be the same size and shape for the instruction to work. It is
also possible to multiply one matrix by another to create a third
matrix, but division cannot be used. Division can be accomplished in another way, however. The instruction MAT B = A/3
will create a new matrix, B, which contains the elements of A
divided by the constant 3.

MAT A = C   Means a new matrix, A, is created which is exactly like an already existing matrix named C. Remember to
DIM matrix A so that it has the same number of rows and columns as C. If A and C do not have the same row and column
pattern only the overlapping segments will be affected by the instruction. If, for example, there is a third row in A but not C the
values of A's third row will stay the same (e.g., will all be 0 if A
has been dimensioned but not used before in the program).

MAT A = TRN(B)   Creates a matrix A whose elements equal
the transposed value of elements in B.

MAT A = INV(B)   Creates a matrix A whose elements equal
the inverse of corresponding B elements. If A(1,2) equals +6
then B(1,2) will equal -6.

Some BASICs also allow a matrix to be redimensioned as
long as the total number of elements does not increase. A(3,2)
has 12 elements. A new matrix that is simply a rearranged A can
be created:

```
10   DIM A(3,2)
20   DIM B(2,3)
30   MAT B = A
```

A, as defined by line 10 creates a 12 element array that looks like this:

$$
\begin{array}{cccc}
1 & 2 & 3 & 4 \\
5 & 6 & 7 & 8 \\
9 & 10 & 11 & 12
\end{array}
$$

The values can be strung out like this:

$$1 \quad 2 \quad 3 \quad 4 \quad 5 \quad 6 \quad 7 \quad 8 \quad 9 \quad 10 \quad 11 \quad 12$$

and reassigned to matrix B.

$$
\begin{array}{ccc}
1 & 2 & 3 \\
4 & 5 & 6 \\
7 & 8 & 9 \\
10 & 11 & 12
\end{array}
$$

If A has more elements than B the elements at the end of A will not be used in creating B. Using a new DIM to reconfigure A, by the way, will not work since matrix variables can only be DIMensioned once per program.

MID$ (string,#,#) and MID (string,#,#)

This function selects a segment of the string specified in the parentheses. The two numbers after the string designation specify the number of characters in the string to be isolated and the point in the string, starting from the left, where selection will begin. It's not really as complicated as it sounds.

```
10  A$ = MYTEST
20  PRINT MID(A$,3,4)
RUN
EST
```

Line 20 says, "Print three characters in string A$ beginning with the fourth character from the left." Generally MID$ works like LEFT$ and the string can either be specified beforehand as in Line 10 above or typed out inside quotation marks as shown below:

20   PRINT MID("MYTEST",3,4)

Conversion — First change MID to MID$ or vice versa. If that doesn't work see LEFT for a conversion model.

N.

Abbreviation for NEXT

NE

Abbreviation for NEW or <> (not equal)

NEX

Abbreviation for NEXT

NEXT

See chapter 7. The only problem you may run into is the use of NEXT with the variable name assumed (NEXT instead of NEXT A, for example) or the assumption of NEXT itself). If you always use NEXT followed by the name of the variable in the FOR statement, there should be no trouble.

NOT

NOT is used in sophisticated IF THEN statements to activate branching instructions when the controlling variable equals 0.

40   IF NOT A THEN 95

Line 40 says "If A equals 0 go to line 95." Conversion is relatively easy. Line 40 could be changed to:

40   IF A = 0 THEN 95

or

40   IF A = 0 GOTO 95

NUM

A function used to determine how many values were entered in the most recent MAT INPUT statement.

10   PRINT NUM

Line 10 will print the size of the last MAT INPUT data set to be printed.

NUMBERS

We normally think of numbers as being just numbers. You already know, however, from chapter 2 that there are numbers, and there are numbers. BASICs use a variety of number formats:

Integer	such as 1, -1, 6432
Floating Point	such as 1.5, -11.621, .0041
Exponential	5.1002E-5, 60E3, 180E-9

See chapter 2 for more information on numbers.

Smaller BASICs may accept only integer or whole numbers but most will accept decimal numbers. Several instructions described in this chapter also provide more details on number formats and advice on conversion.

OCT$(#)

Converts the decimal number in the parentheses to octal. See HEX for more information.

ON G.

Abbreviation for ON GOTO

ON X EXIT #1, #2, #3

Works just like ON RESTORE. See ON RESTORE and EXIT.

ON X RESTORE #1, #2, #3

If X is 1 the next READ takes data from the line specified by the first number (#,). If X is 2 the next READ takes data from line #2, and so on.

ON GOSUB

ON GOSUB is a convenient way of making branching decisions. Here is an example:

10   ON A GOSUB 30,40,50,60

If A equals 1 the computer will branch to 30: if A equals 2 then it branches to 40, and so on. If A is outside the range of 1 to 4 some BASICs just drop through to the next line. Others stop execution and print an error message. See IF GOSUB for more information.

Conversion—ON GOSUB can be simulated with a series of IF GOSUB statements. Just write one for each of the branching options (e.g., IF A = 1 GOSUB 30; IF A = 2 GOSUB 40). If you don't have IF GOSUB to work with it is possible to use IF THEN or IF THEN GOTO. Since GOSUB is designed to branch and then return to the line immediately after the GOSUB, you will have to replace RETURN with a GOTO at the point where the program is to branch back from the subroutine. See IF GOSUB. One potential problem in conversion attempts is the fact that ON GOSUB performs an INT on the controlling variable. In the example above X could equal 1, 1.2, or 1.8, and the computer would branch to line 30. ON GOTO also performs an INT automatically but whatever controlling variable is being used will not be an integer. But if you modify the program so that IF THEN statements are used instead, add an INT to the conversion (IF INT(A) = 1 THEN 30).

Different BASICs permit different numbers of options in ON GOSUBs. Be sure yours allows the number of options required; otherwise try one of the conversions.

ON GOT

Abbreviation for ON GOTO.

ON GOTO

See Chapter 7. This statement works just like ON GOSUB except there is no RETURN and thus no branching back to the main program. See ON GOSUB for some conversion suggestions. One alternative for conversion is shown below:

5   ON N GOTO (110,120,130,140)

can be changed to

5   GOTO 100 + 10*N

This conversion will only work if N multiplied by 10 will produce the "offset" which will be added to the base number (e.g., 100) to get the appropriate line number. INT may have to be used to round off N before multiplying.

OPTION

Used to specify the lowest or base number in an array. OPTION BASE = 0 will cause any array to start with 0 (e.g., A(0), A(1), A(2), etc.) while OPTION BASE = 1 will result in any array to start at 1. Some BASICs may use a form of this statement that does not require the = sign (OPTION BASE 1) but many do not recognize OPTION at all. Instead either 0 or 1 is assumed to be the base number for arrays. See DIM for some conversion suggestions.

OUT

Sends a byte of data to an output port specified in the OUT statement.

10   OUT 01, A

Line 10 sends the ASCII code for A to the port with the assigned address 01. I/O devices such as video displays, printers, serial and parallel ports, and cassette interfaces all have one or more port numbers assigned to them, and these numbers vary from system to system. Many systems do not allow access to the ports via OUT and, instead, use SET commands in the operating system, or some other method for output. BASIC instructions such as LPRINT can often be substituted for OUT. See also the chapters on machine and assembly language programming and USR in this chapter.

OUT #,#

Works exactly like POKE. The first number specifies the memory address where the second number is to be sent. See POKE.

P.

Abbreviation for PRINT.

P.A.

Abbreviation for PRINT AT

PDL

An Apple II BASIC function that controls the operation of game paddles. It would be very difficult to modify programs with PDL.

PEEK #

This statement "reads" the contents of a memory location (specified by the number that follows PEEK).

10   PRINT PEEK 256

Line 10 will print the ASCII equivalent of whatever code is in RAM location 256.

Conversion — EXAM is sometimes used instead of PEEK; otherwise conversion may be a problem.

PI

Stands for 3.14159265. Just use the number or a variable that equals the number instead.

PIN(#)

Works like INP which can be used to replace it where possible (e.g., INP(1) instead of PIN(1)). In some circumstances PEEK might work as a substitute if the port being read is actually a memory address (e.g., in 6502, 6800 computers). The number in parentheses is expressed in decimal form.

PLOT #,#

An APPLE II BASIC graphic instruction. Hard to convert. The first number after PLOT is the column where the small rectangle of color will be displayed; the second number specifies the line. SET serves a similar purpose in the TRS-80 system although only black and white displays are possible. Converting graphics is tedious work which should be done with a copy of the APPLE BASIC manual close at hand.

POINT #

A TRS-80 BASIC statement that tells you if a particular point on the screen grid, specified by the two numbers, is "on" or "off" (e.g., black or white). In Level I a dark point on the screen will produce a 1 and a white spot a 0. Level II produces a -1. Few other BASICs have a comparable statement.

POKE #,#

A very useful statement that is a companion to PEEK. POKE is used to store a value (0-255) in RAM. The number to be stored is the first one; the RAM location as the second.

10   POKE 69,31000

Line 10 puts 69 (45 hex,01000101 binary) in memory location 31,000. FILL or STUFF does the same thing in some versions.

POS(0)

Returns a number that indicates the location of the cursor or print head along the current line. Hard and/or tedious to convert.

PRI

Abbreviation for PRINT.

PRINT

See Chapter 6. In addition to the standard (and normal) uses of PRINT, the TRS-80 computer has a somewhat weird use. PRINT # will record the data that follows the # on the cassette recorder. In Level II the format is PRINT # − 1 if you're using one recorder. PRINT # has a similar use in other BASICs where files (on disk or cassete tape storage) are created and stored. The way this works varies from BASIC to BASIC. A few of the microcomputer BASICs have similar functions for cassette or disk files.

PRINT AT

This special PRINT statement is used in TRS-80 Level I to

specify the specific spot on the screen where printing will commence.

10   PRINT AT 900,"HERE I AM"

Line 10 will print the string "HERE I AM" in the bottom left hand corner of the TRS-80 screen.

Conversion — There are other ways to place the output in a special place on the screen. The best thing to do is decide how your BASIC does it and then get a copy of a TRS-80 screen graph (there's one in the Level I or Level II manual). Use the graph to determine exactly where the material should appear on the screen. In Level II BASIC PRINT AT can be replaced directly by PRINT @.

PRINT "&"

In some BASICs the PRINT statement can be used to generate control functions.

10   PRINT "&C"

The line above will cause the computer to perform the task which is normally accomplished by pressing the control and C key. Here are some common control code functions.

> "&M" — carriage return
> "&J" — line feed
> "&K" — clear screen and home cursor
> "&N" — home cursor

These vary quite a bit from system to system.

PRINT USING

There's a whole nest of PRINT USING statements. Your BASIC may have all, some, or none of them. Generally they can all be simulated by combinations of simpler statements but you should have clearly in mind just what the statement does. Here are some examples:

PRINT USING

This version is handy for printing dollars and cents. The # tells the computer to print the number in a special format. The decimal point will always be in the same spot and only two digits will be printed to the right of the decimal.

```
10   PRINT USING # 6.201
20   PRINT USING # 22.3
30   PRINT USING # 3000
RUN
6.20
22.30
3000.00
```

There are many versions of Print Using that can be selected simply by adding the appropriate symbol or character after PRINT USING. It is possible to insert commas in large values, add a $ at the right place, and generally set up the output in whatever format you desire. Listed below are some sources of additional information for those who need it:

LEVEL II BASIC Reference Manual. This Radio Shack publication provides detailed information on the versions used in LEVEL II BASIC.

Bill Roch, Formatting Numbers in 8K BASIC, *Personal Computing,* August, 1979. This article describes in detail methods for converting PRINT USING statements so they work in less sophisticated BASICs.

If you want a format for printing dollars and cents correctly, see Les Palenik's brief article in the October, 1978 issue of *Byte* entitled "Formatting Dollars and Cents."

Another article on the same topic is "A BASIC dollar edit $ubroutine" by Michael Donahue. It appeared in the November, 1979 issue of *Microcomputing.*

R.

Abbreviation for RUN, RND, or RESET.

RAN

Abbreviation for RANDOMIZE.

RANDOM and RANDOMIZE

Most BASICs will produce an apparently random number using the RND function. These numbers are not really random; indeed they are produced or derived from a "seed" number that then determines the numbers to be generated when a RND function is encountered. RANDOM or RANDOMIZE resets or "reseeds" the random number generator so that a new sequence of numbers will be provided. Some BASICs use RANDOM, some RANDOMIZE; some neither. In the latter case it may be necessary to drop RANDOM or RANDOMIZE completely and adjust the RND sections of the program as well. See RND.

REA

Abbreviation for READ.

READ

See Chapter 6. Very small BASICs may be able to accept only one variable with each READ (e.g., READ A) while most permit multiple variables to be read (e.g., READ A, B, C). If you can't, just break the READ statements into several single variable READ statements. A few Tiny BASICs will not read strings (READ A$). In some cases a string can be read by changing A$ to A. If that doesn't work the only solution may be to buy a bigger BASIC.

Another possible complication is the use of one READ statement to define numeric (e.g., A, B, C...) and string variables (e.g., A$, B$, C$...) If your BASIC doesn't like that, break the READ into two separate statements, one for numeric variables, another for strings. Be sure to adjust DATA statements too.

RES

Abbreviation for RESTORE.

RESET (#,#)

This statement is used in TRS-80 BASICs to create simple graphics. RESET is the opposite of SET. The two numbers in parentheses specify the exact location on the screen where a dot will be "turned off" or made black. SET makes the area white. See SET.

REST.

Abbreviation for RESTORE.

RESTORE

Normally, a READ will begin at the beginning of the first DATA statement and proceed sequentially through the available data. Subsequent READ statements pick up where the previous READ left off. RESTORE has a marked effect on the normal progression of events. Any time a RESTORE is encountered, the next READ will start at the beginning of the first DATA statement. If you don't have RESTORE, it may be possible to make the program work by having it stop using an END statement instead of RESTORE. Then when you type RUN to start again the program will do a RESTORE automatically. If starting at the beginning of the program everytime is a problem, insert some sort of jump (e.g., IF $X = 2$ GOTO 640) that allows you to skip to the proper point in the program each time.

One variation in the RESTORE statement thay may cause trouble is the use of specific line numbers after RESTORE. RESTORE 60 affects only the data in line 60. Most BASICs won't understand this variation, but if all that data is in one line you need do no more than drop the reference to a specific line. If data is spread over several lines, you may have to reset all the lines and then use dummy variables to get back to the desired position in the DATA line that should not have been affected. For example, if you have read three numbers in line 80 when a RESTORE sets the "pointer" back to the beginning of the line, you could have the program read D1, D2, and D3 (dummy variables that will never be used). That will bring you back to the desired place in the DATA line.

RESUME

SAME AS CONT

RET and RET.

Abbreviation for RETURN.

RETURN

See Chapter 7.

RIGHT(string,#) and RIGHT$(string,#)

This function is used to isolate a particular segment of a string. The string to be used is specified first in the parentheses and the number following indicates the number of characters to be isolated.

```
10  A$ = "MAH STRING"
20  PRINT RIGHT$(A$,6)
RUN
STRING
```

The program above prints the rightmost six characters of the string "MAH STRING."

Conversion — It would be difficult to find a suitable substitute for this function, but in many cases it is not an essential part of the program. See LEFT$ and MID$ for conversion information.

RND

See Chapter 7. This is often used to provide the program with an unpredictable number. In some computers RND is used with no argument following it. Each time a RND is processed, a new or different number is provided. Other BASICs use an argument (e.g., RND(0), RND(6), and so on). It may make a difference whether the number in parentheses is positive, negative, or 0. Often RND(0), when used over and over, will produce the same number each time. If you need that capability but don't have it, just assign a name to the RND number the first time it is used (e.g., R = RND(0)), and replace future RND(0)'s with the name you assigned to it (R in this case).

Almost all BASICs will produce a number between 0 and 1 (e.g., .603420, .100123, .999628) and you must process those numbers further to generate numbers within some other range such as from 0 to 9 or 1 to 21. This process is described in Chapter 7. Radio Shack's BASIC, however, does all that for you by having the maximum number to be produced specified in the parentheses:

```
10  PRINT RND(21)
```

will produce a number somewhere between 1 and 21 with 1 being the lowest possible number and 21 the highest. Other versions will require several lines of instructions to accomplish the same thing as line 10. Again, see Chapter 7. One final note. A few BASICs use RND as an abbreviation for RANDOM. See RANDOM.

S.

Abbreviation for STEP, SET, or STOP depending on the context. If it is in a FOR NEXT loop it means STEP (e.g., S. −1), if there are two numbers after it (S. (27,120)) it means SET.

SCRN(#,#)

An Apple BASIC statement that is used to read the color of the screen at a particular location. Each color has a different number.

```
10   PRINT SCRN(13,21)
```

Line 10 looks at a screen location specified by the two numbers in parentheses and determines what color is displayed. That color's number is then printed.

Conversion—This particular function is unique to the Apple. In many cases, however, if you can figure out what purpose is served by SCRN, it will be possible to rewrite the program and use the features of your BASIC.

SEARCH A$,B$,C

Searches string two (B$) for the first occurrence of A$. The location of A$ in B$ is then assigned to C. Here is an example:

```
10   A$ = "DEF"
20   B$ = "ABCDEFGHI"
30   SEARCH A$,B$,C
40   PRINT C
RUN
4
```

A four was printed because the substring "DEF" is found in B$ beginning with the fourth character or position in B$. If DEF

had not been a part of B$, C would have equaled 0. Conversion
of SEARCH is possible but difficult. This is often used in computer assisted instruction to match the answer with the response
of the student. A CAI program that uses SEARCH often could
probably be written in PILOT more efficiently. When
SEARCH is used only once in a program and is necessary for
the program to work, it can be simulated by some of the string
functions such as LEFT, RIGHT, MID. Use them or their
equivalents in a FOR NEXT loop to compare each segment of
the B$ with A$.

SEG$ (string,#,#)

The equivalent if MID$ in TI BASIC. Here is an example:

```
 5   A$ = "MAH STRING"
10   PRINT SEG(A$,4,3)
RUN
ING
```

SEG$ selects a substring or section of the string specified in the
parentheses. In line 10 the substring began with the fourth character from the left and included three characters.

SET (#,#)

The TRS-80 computer divides its screen into a series of blocks
with each block having a unique address. The address has two
numbers which specify the horizontal and vertical position. SET
"turns on" a specified block. That is, it makes it white. RESET
works the same way but makes a block dark. See RESET for
more information.

SET DS =

Sets display speed from fast (0) to very slow (99). A specialized instruction that may or may not have a counterpart in your
BASIC. When absolutely necessary some of the functions of
this command could be simulated with a FOR NEXT loop that
does some time-consuming computational task.

SET·IP =

Sets output port by number. Works same as the SOLOS operating system command described in chapter 3. See OUT also.

SET LL =

Sets length of lines output from BASIC program. In BASICs where this is possible the exact method of accomplishing it varies considerably.

SET ML =

Tells BASIC not to use memory above #. Many versions of BASIC permit you to "protect" a certain area of memory. The TRS-80, for example, asks for a protected memory address each time the system is powered up. Check your manual.

SGN(X)

Returns 1 of X is positive, − 1 if X is negative and 0 if X is zero.

SIN(#)

Computes the sine of angle A with the number in parentheses expressed in radians. If you want degrees instead of radians then multiply radians by 57.2578. If you need to convert degrees to radians multiply degrees by .0174533. See Log Functions.

SLEEP

Does just what it says. Puts the computer to sleep (has it pause) for a time specified by the number following SLEEP. The number gives the rest time in tenths of a second.

```
10   SLEEP 100
```

Statement 10 makes the computer pause for 10 seconds. If you have PAUSE (e.g., P.T. Extended BASIC), it can replace SLEEP or WAIT. If you have no suitable replacement it is still possible to make the computer pause for a while by executing a time consuming but pointless FOR NEXT loop. The simplest is just an empty loop:

```
10   FOR E = 1 to 10000
20   NEXT E
```

You can time the execution of this loop and adjust it to obtain whatever pause you need. If a pause is called for in several places it is best to write a short subroutine and access it whenever necessary with GOSUB. More time will be consumed in the loop if computations are added. Adding the line below to the model above would slow it down considerably:

$$15 \quad A = E*E/E + E\hat{\ }E$$

Be careful, however, that the computation does not involve numbers that are outside the range accepted by the computer.

SPA(#) or SPACES(#) or SPC(#)

This function produces a series of spaces.

```
20  PRINT SPACE(5) "NEW PARAGRAPH"
RUN
          NEW PARAGRAPH
```

The computer moved over five spaces before printing the string.

Conversion—If you're lucky, one of the variations (SPA, SPACES$, SPC) will work for you. If not try using TAB (see Chapter 7) instead. TAB moves the cursor or print head to a specified location on the line and will usually serve the same purpose. If TAB isn't suitable or is unavailable it is possible to obtain spaces by enclosing them in quotation marks.

```
10  PRINT "OLD PARAGRAPH"
20  PRINT "               NEW PARAGRAPH"
```

SQR(#) or SQRT(#)

This function computes the square root of a positive number in the parentheses.

```
10  PRINT SQR(81)
RUN
9
```

ST

Abbreviation of STEP

ST, and STE

Abbreviation of STOP.

STEP and STE

See Chapter 7. A simple FOR NEXT loop, with no STEP specified, will increment the variable in the FOR statement by one each time the loop is executed. If STEP is also available you will also be able to make the computer increment the FOR NEXT variable by some positive number other than one (e.g., 2, 6, or 7).

If you get any fancier with STEP, many of the simpler BASICs will not understand. Some STEPs use negative numbers, (STEP -4), some decimal (STEP .56) and some use variables (STEP A).

Conversion — It is possible to simulate the STEP by adding a line of instruction to the program just before the NEXT instruction. Here is an example:

```
10   FOR X = 1 TO 10 STEP 3
20   PRINT "WHAT! AGAIN?";
30   PRINT X
40   NEXT X
```

Lines 10 through 40 will generate the following output:

```
What! Again? 1
What! Again? 4
What! Again? 7
What! Again? 10
```

The same output can be produced without the STEP.

```
10   FOR X = 1 TO 10
20   PRINT "WHAT! AGAIN?";
30   PRINT X
35   X = (X - 1) + 3
40   NEXT X
```

In the second example line 35 serves the same purpose as STEP 3. As shown, it is a little more complicated than necessary. Instead of $(X - 1) + 3$ it should be written $X + 2$. The longer form was used to illustrate the process. The -1 which is subracted will adjust for the -1 that will automatically be added to X each time the program goes through the FOR NEXT loop. Then 3 was added to X just as it would be if STEP 3 were placed at the end of line 10.

STO

Abbreviation for STOP

STOP

STOP tells the computer to stop executing the program. END serves a similar purpose but STOP is usually intended to be temporary. In most BASICs the program can be continued from the point where it stopped by typing CONTINUE or CONT.

Conversion — Determine the purpose of STOP in the program. It may be possible to remove it without drastically affecting operation. In other cases substituting END may work, or insert a GOTO that sends the program to a line that then prints out a message telling what has happened and use some other method (e.g., an INPUT) to halt execution temporarily.

STR$(#)

This function converts a number to a string. That may sound silly at first but there are some functions that will work only on strings. If you need to use one of them on a number, STR$(#) will do the trick. The number in parentheses is then treated as a string. See VAL and CONVERT also.

STRING$(#,character code)

This handy function will print the character whose ASCII code is specified inside the parentheses as many times as is indicated by the first number in the parentheses.

```
10   PRINT STRING(8,46)
RUN
. . . . . . . .
```

The ASCII decimal code for a period is 46. You may be able to avoid using the ASCII code for a character by inclosing the character itself in quotes instead.

10 PRINT STRING$(8,".")

These two lines do the same thing: It would also be possible to use a regular PRINT statement to accomplish the same thing.

10 PRINT "........"

Strings

See Chapters 6 and 7. There are two traditions in string handling — one going back to HP BASIC, the other to DEC BASIC. The HP approach was adopted by Data General and Northstar, while DEC was emulated by MITS, MicroSoft, and all the BASICs that are copied or legitimately derived from Microsoft.

PRINT MID$(A$,2,3) is a DEC style function that says "print a substring that begins at location 2 in string A$ and is 3 characters long." The same thing would be accomplished, HP Style, this way — "PRINT A$(2,3)." DEC derivatives use RIGHT and LEFT, HP doesn't:

10 PRINT RIGHT$(S$,3)
10 PRINT S$(3)

Both line 10's say "Print the rightmost three characters in string S."

20 PRINT LEFT$(S$,3)
20 PRINT S$(1,3)

Both line 20's say "Print the leftmost three characters, beginning with the first character, and ending with the third from the left." In DEC BASIC + RIGHT(S$,3) means "start with the third character from the left and print everything from there to the rightmost extreme of the string." In MITS BASIC it means "print the last three characters on the right of string S."

HP type BASICs also need a DIM for strings; DEC type BASICs do not.

STUFF #,#

This statement puts the second number in a memory location specified by the first.

Conversion — See POKE or FILL

SYSTEM and SYS

Some computers use this command to leave BASIC and enter the operating system software. Other computers leave BASIC when the word BYE or when the ASCII code for "CONTROL C", the ESCAPE key, is encountered.

Generally the appearance of any of these in a program means machine language instructions are coming — converting will involve changing or adapting that too — a job you may not want to tackle till you have a little experience under your belt.

T.

Abbreviation for TAB or THEN.

TAB

See Chapter 7. Almost every BASIC has TAB, but if yours doesn't, try using PRINT statements with spaces where the TAB should be. Essentially, TAB works like the tab key on a typewriter. TAB followed by a number, such as TAB(45), moves the cursor over to that location on the line.

```
10  PRINT TAB(5)"TABBED 5";TAB(25)"TABBED 25"
RUN
      TABBED 5                 TABBED 25
```

The first string (TABBED 5) was printed on the line from position 5 on. The second string was printed from position 25 on.

TAN(#)

Computes the tangent of the angle in the parentheses. The answer is in radians. Lee Log Functions.

TEXT

In Apple II BASIC this statement will cause the computer to stop operating in the graphics mode and resume regular operation — that is, print letters and numbers instead of graphics symbols. TEXT in some BASICs defines the variables that follow as strings (e.g., TEXT A,B).

Conversion — An Apple program with TEXT will require considerable modification to duplicate the graphics. Do it only with considerable knowledge of your BASIC and Apple II. If TEXT defines the variable as a string it is an entirely different matter. Changing A to A$, B to B$, and so on should eliminate the need for TEXT, but you may have to add appropriate DIM statements if the strings will be longer than the default value for strings in your system.

THE

Abbreviation for THEN.

THEN

See Chapter 6.

TI

Abbreviation for TIME.

TIM or TIME or TIME$ or TI$

These keep track of the amount of time a program has consumed.

10   PRINT TIM

Line 10 should print out the number of minutes you've been running a program.

Conversion — It would be difficult for a beginner to handle converting programs that require TIME or TIME$. On the big machines these functions are used to print out the time when someone signs on and off the timesharing console. On microprocessors the functions usually count elapsed time, although the meaning of the number produced varies. It could be based on "60ths" of a second (e.g., 60 units + 1 second in the PET) or some other value. If you have a similar function in your BASIC it may be possible to adjust the base with a minimum of effort. This tends to be a specialized function that is tailored to a particular system.

TUOFF

Turns off the relay switch that controls whether the motor on the cassette recorder is running.

TUON

Turns on the relay switch that controls the operation of the motor on the cassette recorder. When TUON is executed, the recorder will start.

TYP(0)

Returns either 1, 2, or 3 depending on whether the next DATA value is numeric (1), a string (2) or nothing (3). A 3 means there is no more data in the DATA statement.

10   PRINT TYP(0)

When line 10 is executed the computer will find the next DATA value, that is, the one which would be used next if a READ were executed. A 1 indicates the next DATA value is numeric, a 2 indicates the next DATA value is a string, and a 3 means there is no more DATA available.

USR

This statement is used in several BASICs to interface a BASIC program with a machine language program. The machine language program may be some frequently used routine that is slow in BASIC but fast if done in machine language. Or it may be a subroutine that is used to output or input data to or from a peripheral. Frequently the machine language program itself will be placed in a particular section of memory by the BASIC program using PEEK or it may be placed in memory using the monitor commands. In my own system I have a machine language I/O routine for a Selectric typewriter printer. It is stored on cassette and loaded into memory at a convenient spot. Then when a BASIC program needs it the USR function is a handy way to get access to it. See Chapters 4 and 5.

VAL

Used to reconvert numbers that were made into strings by

STR. If A was the number 622, and it was converted to a string it will be necessary to use VAL before treating A as a numeric value again.

40   VAL(A$)

Some BASICs, such as TRS-80 level II, will accept a mixed string and isolate the number component if it comes first.

```
10   A$ = "10 dollars"
20   VAL(A$)
30   PRINT A
RUN
10
```

VAL, as used above, is a sophisticated version many BASICs lack. Rewriting the original string so it isn't mixed (e.g., drop "dollars" in line 10) may be your only recourse.

VARPTR(#)

This function gives the memory address of a variable. If, for example, the data for array A was stored in memory beginning at address 16324 then

10   PRINT VARPTR(A(0))

would produce 16324. Conversion would be difficult.

VLIN #,# AT

This is a specialized statement in Apple II BASIC that allows a vertical line to be drawn at a particular point on the screen. The first two numbers tell the computer how long and where in the vertical plane the line will be. The third number tells the column in which to draw the line. Conversion is possible, but you must know exactly what is to appear on the screen and make use of whatever graphics or standard print features your system has to accomplish the same thing.

VTAB

The Apple computer can display 24 lines on the screen at one time. If you want to print something on a particular line VTAB will do that for you. VTAB 1 says print whatever comes next on the first line at the top of the screen while VTAB 24 begins printing at the very bottom of the screen.

Conversion—PRINT AT, if you have it, can be an effective substitute. Just determine the address of the beginning space on the line where the material is to be printed. You could also use a series of PRINT statements to move to the desired position. CLEAR or CLS can help to. See CURSOR also.

WAIT

In some BASICs WAIT works the same as PAUSE. WAIT 100 usually makes the computer pause for 100 seconds. In other BASICs, the units referred to may be fractions of seconds. For example, if the unit referred to is ½ second, then WAIT 100 would mean that the computer would pause for 50 seconds (100 half-seconds). See PAUSE for conversion suggestions.

WAIT #,#,#

This special function tells the computer to pause or stop executing the current program. While it is waiting, the computer looks at the input port whose number is the same as the first number following WAIT. The computer takes whatever value is present on the input port specified and ANDs it with the value specified by the middle number. When the result of that AND equals the value specified by the last number, the computer ends its pause and begins processing instructions again. Complicated, isn't it?

XOR

A logic function, often referred to as "Exclusive Or". When an "Exclusive Or", or XOR, is performed, the result is similar to the OR function except when the two signals are both 1. For example, consider the command

PRINT A XOR B

In this case, if A is 1 and B is 0, the result will be 1, just as with the OR function. If, however, both A and B are 1, the result will be 0 in contrast to the 1 which results from the OR function. See Chapter 2.

SYMBOLS AND PUNCTUATION MARKS

[ ]

Some computers use brackets in place of parentheses. Replace [ ] with ( ) if your BASIC doesn't use brackets.

@

See PRINT @

#

When this sign is added to a number it designates it as double precision rather than single precision. That means numbers are stored in an extended format accurate to 17 digits. When the number is printed, only 16 digits will appear in the display. See ! for an explanation of single precision. See Chapter 2 also.

```
10   A = 5.2
20   B = 6.1
30   C# = B/A
40   PRINT C#
RUN
1.173076987266541
```

produces a more accurate number. In some programs you may be able to get along without it, but for many financial and statistical applications it will not be possible to achieve the necessary level of accuracy without some form of extended precision. See DBL and CDBL for more information.

is also used in place of PRINT in some BASICs, and a few use it instead of <> or "not equal". PRINT USING may also have the # as a modifier.

```
10   A = 5.2
20   PRINT USING "##.##"; A
RUN
 5.20
```

The #'s specify the format — in this case at least two numbers before the decimal and two after. If there aren't enough numbers, zeros are added automatically on the right of the decimal point with spaces added on the left. In our example there is a space to the left of the 5.

Finally the # is used in some BASICs as part of routines that move data to and from files. If you have more than one cassette, disk, or printer, statements like READ may be written READ#2, which tells the computer which of several devices is to be used. Conversions involve rewriting the program to fit your system (e.g., changing from two disk drives to two cassettes). You should know the names c numbers assigned to each of the various I/O options on your system and understand the method used to select I/O devices for output.

$

See Chapters 6 and 7. When added to a letter (A$) it signifies that A is the name of a string variable. Strings are handled similarly by most BASICs, but some vary in the maximum length of string they will accept. See also DIM and Chapter 7.

!

Sometimes an abbreviation for REMARK. ! is also used to change a double precision number (17 digits accurate) into a less precise single precision number. Single precision stores only seven digits (it prints six digits) and conserves memory. In fact, single precision is the "default" format for BASIC and you have to use something like DEFDLE to get double precision. See CSNG.

! is also sometimes a part of a PRINT USING statement where it tells the computer to print only the leftmost character in a string.

```
10   A$ = "APPLE":B$ = "DOG":C$ = "GRANDMOTHER"
20   PRINT USING "!";A$;B$;C$
RUN
ADG
```

"%"

Defines a number as an integer.

```
10  A = 2.6
20  PRINT A%,
RUN
2
```

See INT for a possible substitute. The %, may also be used in some PRINT USING statements as a modifier.

?

Abbreviation for PRINT.

\

Some BASICs use the backslash instead of the colon (:) to separate multiple statements on one line. Your BASIC probably uses : instead. Don't confuse it with / which is the division symbol. If neither \ nor : work, put all the statement on separate lines.

** or ^ or ↑

Used for exponentiation.

```
10  PRINT 2**3
20  PRINT 3^3
RUN
8
27
```

Line 10 reads "Print 2 to the 3rd power." Try Λ if your BASIC doesn't take ** or ^ or ↑. If you don't have any, use this substitution:

```
10  PRINT 2*2*2
20  PRINT 3*3*3
RUN
8
27
```

Remember that roots may be obtained with ↑ or its equivalent.

```
10   PRINT 25↑(½)
RUN
5
```

Line 10 computes the square root of 25. Replace the ½ in parentheses with a ⅓ and you will get the cube root. You can also use decimal numbers (i.e., .5 or .33) instead of fractions to designate the root in terms of an expression of power. Remember to use the parentheses when using fractions. 25↑½ means 25 raised to the first power, then divided by 2, or 12½. 25↑(½) means 25 raised to the ½ power, or 5.

+

In addition to the standard use of the plus sign to signify the addition of numbers, some, but by no means all, BASICs use the + to add together strings.

```
10   A$ = "FOAT"
20   B$ = "WUTH"
30   PRINT A$ + b$
RUN
FOAT WUTH
```

The plus sign may also stand for a logic OR operation. Here is an example:

```
10   IF (A = 6) + (B>4) THEN 30
```

Line 10 says, "If A is equal to 6 or if B is greater than 4 then jump to line 30".

*

Signifies multiplication in most cases, but it can also indicate a logic AND function.

```
10   IF (A = 6)*(B>4) THEN 30
```

Line 10 says, "If A is equal to 6 and if B is also greater than 4 then jump to line 30."

=

In addition to its use in mathematical comparisons and equations, = is used to compare strings in some BASICs. If your BASIC can't compare strings, you may be able to substitute numbers in the program for the offending strings, but don't bet the ranch on it. The rewriting may be extensive.

< > and their friends

It is possible to combine <, > and = in different ways to make several different sorts of comparisons. The use of these in mathematical comparisons was considered in Chapter 7. These comparators can also be used, in some BASICs, to compare strings. String comparisons work a little oddly though. Here are some explanatory examples:

```
10   A$ = "AB"
20   B$ = "ABC"
30   IF A$<B$ THEN 50
```

If the program above were run it would skip to line 50 because B$ has one more letter than A$. But look at this one:

```
10   A$ = "HI"
20   B$ = "HELLO"
30   IF A$<B$ THEN 50
```

It would seem clear that A$ is "less than" B$ but that isn't true. In actual fact the comparison is made letter by letter in terms of the ASCII code that stands for that letter. In the program, both A$ and B$ have H as the first character. H has a decimal ASCII code of 72. The next letter in A$ is I which has an ASCII code of 73. B$ has E as its second letter, and E has a code of 69. Since 69 is less than 73 that means E is less than I and B$ is "less than" A$. Since A$ must be less than B$ if line 30 is to produce a jump to line 50, it will not occur. If your computer will compare strings but doesn't seem to work properly in a particular program, it may be because the strings to be compared are too long for your BASIC. If possible, use some of the string functions to cut down without losing meaningful data.

Some BASICs use peculiar symbols in making numeric or string comparisons. # may be used instead of ><; or <> may replace ><. Some may understand =< but not <= or vice versa. <= is the same as =< (equal to or less than), and >= is the same as => (greater than or equal to). =/ may be the same as <> or "not equal to."

The apostrophe is an abbreviation for REMARK, and may be used instead of " " to enclose strings.

Appendix

Conversion Table

Base Conversion Table

BIN	OCT	DEC	HEX	BIN	OCT	DEC	HEX
0	0	0	00	100010	42	34	22
1	1	1	01	100011	43	35	23
10	2	2	02	100100	44	36	24
11	3	3	03	100101	45	37	25
100	4	4	04	100110	46	38	26
101	5	5	05	100111	47	39	27
110	6	6	06	101000	50	40	28
111	7	7	07	101001	51	41	29
1000	10	8	08	101010	52	42	2A
1001	11	9	09	101011	53	43	2B
1010	12	10	0A	101100	54	44	2C
1011	13	11	0B	101101	55	45	2D
1100	14	12	0C	101110	56	46	2E
1101	15	13	0D	101111	57	47	2F
1110	16	14	0E	110000	60	48	30
1111	17	15	0F	110001	61	49	31
10000	20	16	10	110010	62	50	32
10001	21	17	11	110011	63	51	33
10010	22	18	12	110100	64	52	34
10011	23	19	13	110101	65	53	35
10100	24	20	14	110110	66	54	36
10101	25	21	15	110111	67	55	37
10110	26	22	16	111000	70	56	38
10111	27	23	17	111001	71	57	39
11000	30	24	18	111010	72	58	3A
11001	31	25	19	111011	73	59	3B
11010	32	26	1A	111100	74	60	3C
11011	33	27	1B	111101	75	61	3D
11100	34	28	1C	111110	76	62	3E
11101	35	29	1D	111111	77	63	3F
11110	36	30	1E	1000000	100	64	40
11111	37	31	1F	1000001	101	65	41
100000	40	32	20	1000010	102	66	42
100001	41	33	21	1000011	103	67	43

BIN	OCT	DEC	HEX	BIN	OCT	DEC	HEX
1000100	104	68	44	1111110	176	126	7E
1000101	105	69	45	1111111	177	127	7F
100110	106	70	46	10000000	200	128	80
100111	107	71	47	10000001	201	129	81
1001000	110	72	48	10000010	202	130	82
1001001	111	73	49	10000011	203	131	83
1001010	112	74	4A	10000100	204	132	84
1001011	113	75	4B	10000101	205	133	85
1001100	114	76	4C	10000110	206	134	86
1001101	115	77	4D	10000111	207	135	87
1001110	116	78	4E	10001000	210	136	88
1001111	117	79	4F	10001001	211	137	89
1010000	120	80	50	10001010	212	138	8A
1010001	121	81	51	10001011	213	139	8B
1010010	112	82	52	10001100	214	140	8C
1010011	123	83	53	10001101	215	141	8D
1010100	124	84	54	10001110	216	142	8E
1010101	125	85	55	10001111	217	143	8F
1010110	126	86	56	10010000	220	144	90
1010111	127	87	57	10010001	221	145	91
1011000	130	88	58	10010010	222	146	92
1011001	131	89	59	10010011	223	147	93
1011010	132	90	5A	10010100	224	148	94
1011011	133	91	5B	10010101	225	149	95
1011100	134	92	5C	10010110	226	150	96
1011101	135	93	5D	10010111	227	151	97
1011110	136	94	5E	10011000	230	152	98
1011111	137	95	5F	10011001	231	153	99
1100000	140	96	60	10011010	232	154	9A
1100001	141	97	61	10011011	223	155	9B
1100010	142	98	62	10011100	234	156	9C
1100011	143	99	63	10011101	235	157	9D
1100100	144	100	64	10011110	236	158	9E
1100101	145	101	65	10011111	237	159	9F
1100110	146	102	66	10100000	240	160	A0
1100111	147	103	67	10100001	241	161	A1
1101000	150	104	68	10100010	242	162	A2
1101001	151	105	69	10100011	243	163	A3
1101010	152	106	6A	10100100	244	164	A4
1101011	153	107	6B	10100101	245	165	A5
1101100	154	108	6C	10100110	246	166	A6
1101101	155	109	6D	10100111	247	167	A7
1101110	156	110	6E	10101000	250	168	A8
1101111	157	111	6F	10101001	251	169	A9
1110000	160	112	70	10101010	252	170	AA
1110001	161	113	71	10101011	253	171	AB
1110010	162	114	72	10101100	254	172	AC
1110011	163	115	73	10101101	255	173	AD
1110100	164	116	74	10101110	256	174	AE
1110101	165	117	75	10101111	257	175	AF
1110110	166	118	76	10110000	260	176	B0
1110111	167	119	77	10110001	261	177	B1
1111000	170	120	78	10110010	262	178	B2
1111001	171	121	79	10110011	263	179	B3
1111010	172	122	7A	10110100	264	180	B4
1111011	173	123	7B	10110101	265	181	B5
1111100	174	124	7C	10110110	266	182	B6
1111101	175	125	7D	10110111	267	183	B7

BIN	OCT	DEC	HEX	BIN	OCT	DEC	HEX
10111000	270	184	B8	11011100	334	220	DC
10111001	271	185	Ь9	11011101	335	221	DD
10111010	272	186	BA	11011110	336	222	DE
10111011	273	187	BB	11011111	337	223	DF
10111100	274	188	BC	11100000	340	224	E0
10111101	275	189	BD	11100001	341	225	E1
10111110	276	190	BD	11100010	342	226	E2
10111111	277	191	BF	11100011	343	227	E3
11000000	300	192	C0	11100100	344	228	E4
11000001	301	193	C1	11100101	345	229	E5
11000010	302	194	C2	11100110	346	230	E6
11000011	303	195	C3	11100111	347	231	E7
11000100	304	196	C4	11101000	350	232	E8
11000101	305	197	C5	11101001	351	233	E9
11000110	306	198	C6	11101010	352	234	EA
11000111	307	199	C7	11101011	353	235	EB
11001000	310	200	C8	11101100	354	236	EC
11001001	311	201	C9	11101101	355	237	ED
11001010	312	202	CA	11101110	356	238	EE
11001011	313	203	CB	11101111	357	239	EF
11001100	314	204	CC	11110000	360	240	F0
11001101	315	205	CD	11110001	361	241	F1
11001110	316	206	CE	11110010	362	242	F2
11001111	317	207	CF	11110011	363	243	F3
11010000	320	208	D0	11110100	364	244	F4
11010001	321	209	D1	11110101	365	245	F5
11010010	322	210	D2	11110110	366	246	F6
11010011	323	211	D3	11110111	367	247	F7
11010100	324	212	D4	11111000	370	248	F8
11010101	325	213	D5	11111001	371	249	F9
11010110	326	214	D6	11111010	372	250	FA
11010111	327	215	D7	11111011	373	251	FB
11011000	330	216	D8	11111100	374	252	FC
11011001	331	217	D9	11111101	375	253	FD
11011010	332	218	DA	11111110	376	254	FE
11011011	333	219	DB	11111111	377	255	FF

Index